YOUR PERSONAL BEHAVIOR MAP TO SELF-FULFILLMENT

A Book For All Families As Life Lessons From A Teacher, Coach And Parent

HARVEY D. HEARTLEY, SR.

Foreword by Dean Smith

Your Personal Behavior Map To Self-Fulfillment

A Book For All Families As Life Lessons From A Coach, Teacher, And Parent

This reprinted and reissued edition is the work of Harvey D. Heartley, Sr. as brought back into print by his son, Harvey D. Heartley, Jr. Preface by Maria L. Heartley, Forward by Dean Smith

Published by:
Lee Ann and Veronica's Publishing
(An imprint of Righteous Pen Publications)
http://apenandadream.righteouspenpublications.com

All rights reserved. No part of this book may be reproduced or transmitted in any form or by any means, electronic or mechanical, or information storage and retrieval system without written permission from the author.

All contents are the thoughts and opinions of the author, and are not those of the publisher, its employees, or the publisher's other authors.

All Bible passages are taken from the **Holy Bible, Authorized King James Version,** Public Domain.

Copyright © 2015 by Harvey D. Heartley, Jr.

ISBN: 1940197295
13-Digit: 978-1-940197-29-6

Printed in the United States of America.

Dedication

This book is dedicated to my wife, Maria, and my four lovely children (Delphyne, Harvey Jr., Shawn, and Gregory); the late, great basketball coach and my mentor, Dr. John B. McLendon; all of my family members (especially my mother, father, and brothers), past, present, and future; and all of my fellow coaches, players, co-workers, students, and friends who have taught me most of the lessons found in this book. It is also dedicated to the St. Augustine's University family, which gave me the opportunity to grow and help contribute to the university, the community, and the nation. I have the deepest love and appreciation for you all, and I truly love you all!

Table Of Contents

	Preface (by Maria Heartley)	7
	Foreword (by Dean Smith)	9
	Introduction	11
1	Basic Guidelines For Life	23
	The <u>Real</u> Daily Dozen: Life's Twelve Developmental Tasks	
2	Attitude	33
3	Relationships	53
4	Imagination	69
5	Socializing	83
6	Education	95
7	Mentality	109
8	Physical Fitness	121
9	Finances	131
10	Professionalism	149
11	Politics	175
12	Sexuality	189
13	Spirituality	201
14	Making It All Work Together	217
	Conclusion	219
	Recommended Reading	223
	About The Author	225

PREFACE

HARVEY Heartley has written a most inspiring personal treatise, filled with humor and wit. His book, *Your Personal Behavior Map To Self-Fulfillment: A Book For All Families As Life Lessons From A Coach, Teacher, And Parent* is the result of a lifetime of personal study and application of genuine wisdom. In this creative work, he engages in the process of personal development, both of himself and the reader. This interactive style is the result of his experiences as a world traveler, social leader, political mediator, civic organizer, financial advisor, motivational lecturer, recreational icon, and astute mentor. Harvey's conversational tone makes the reading enjoyable and has a wide audience appeal.

This book has been an ongoing process over a number of years, 20 twenty years I have known and been married to him. His adoring children also have benefited from his guidance and wisdom. The work is genuinely "Harvey Heartley," for he speaks from the heart. Harvey lets the reader in on his secrets for living a wholesome and productive life. Families, without regard to race, creed, class, or nationality, will enjoy this book, which shares generational wisdom. His philosophy of life is that "attitude determines altitude." Therefore, it is necessary to maintain a positive outlook on life, which radiates from within to the world without. He uses artistic license to call this comprehensive philosophy "SEMPP-FAR-SIS," which is an acronym for "Spirituality, Physical fitness, Education, Mentality, Politics, Professionalism, Finances, Attitude, Relationships, Sociality, Imagination, and Sexuality."

All of the aforementioned attributes have been deeply etched upon his character and have given him a healthful perspective on life. The outflow is what he calls his infinite processing and is what gives the book its particular and universal appeal. It is a great contribution to the personal essay genre.

Loving wife,
Maria L. Heartley

FOREWORD

*Y**OUR Personal Behavior Map to Self-Fulfillment: A Book For All Families As Life Lessons From A Coach, Teacher, And Parent* is a great testimony to Coach Harvey Heartley, a man I have known for over 30 years as a man of honest character and integrity. His 12 life lessons give enlightening and practical perspectives on fundamental issues we all face in the course of living. It is well-worth reading.

In these challenging days of family uncertainties, Coach Heartley gives detailed explanations and suggestions as to how to master problems that have existed over time. These same issues will persist in the future, regardless of race, culture or ethnic backgrounds.

I highly recommend this book for every individual to read and share with his or her families, friends and co-workers. It is an excellent book with a unique, sound approach to winning in life. Coach Heartley's suggestions are sensible and applicable to all people in any aspect of life.

Congratulations, Coach, on this distinguished achievement.

Dean Smith
Basketball Coach Emeritus
The University of North Carolina

Introduction

DO WHAT YOU CAN, WITH WHAT YOU HAVE, WHERE YOU ARE, NOW!

I have always written things down. When I coached basketball teams, I kept a log of each game as it went along. People would say to me, "What are you doing, sitting over there writing during the game?" I wrote down every aspect of the game: the names of the members of the opposing team and the names of our players; our defensive and offensive plans; the heights and weights of each team players, and their relative strengths and weaknesses; the officials (in case I needed to second guess them), etc. and then I documented every play of each game. At timeouts and at the half, I would relate to our players exactly what had happened in the game thus far and, based on those observations, I would diagram the plays and tell them what our strategy would be for the second half. At the end of each game, whether we won or lost, I would write it all up while it was fresh in my mind. This gave me something to study before the next time we played them. I literally kept a dairy of all my coaching experiences, and learned from each one of them. I did the same thing in other areas of my life. Each month, I tried to look back over the previous month and understand what was good and what was not. Now I do it each night and every morning when I wake up. At this stage of my life, I don't write as much down, but every morning when I wake up, I think about what I did yesterday: what was good or bad, and what I am going to do today. I keep a daily schedule of what I need to get done.

Even with all the planning and reflection, life is often a paradox. No matter how well I plan, there are always things that will throw my plans off kilter. I know that there is no perfect way to live my life, but I have found ways to enable myself to function at my best, and I shared my experiences and life lessons with countless others over the years. Family, friends, students, co-workers, and several fellow coaches have encouraged me to "put all of this together in a book." Former students have come back to see me years after they graduated and said, "Remember that day you told us…It struck a chord for me then, and you really got me started…" and they will relate some lessons I passed on to them. Most of the time, I would have completely forgotten the incident. Two experiences that occurred many years apart made me decide to write this book and formalize these life lessons. First, when my mother died in 1986 and we held the celebration of her life, I realized the extent to which she had affected the lives of so many people. When my father died ten years later, we found a big file cabinet with history of the family and also history of our church. It had information about my great-grandparents and many of our other relatives. Because this history was written down, we were able to pass it from one generation to the next. On October 16, 2000, my wife and I attended the Million Family March in Washington, DC. I looked around at the thousands of people of all ages, backgrounds and religions. It occurred to me that we all shared something in common: we were all searching for some answers in our family lives today. That weekend, as I walked around, listened, and spoke to people there, I realized that the great gift I had been given: wise and caring parents, grandparents and a loving wife who helped me in my own life philosophies and beliefs. I realized what I had should be shared with the many others who may not have had the benefits I had. So this is the legacy that I want to share with my family, friends, all my students, my athletes and those many readers whom I have never met personally, but who could use some insight and guidance in this difficult but wonderful thing we call living.

- **This is not a typical self-help book.** There are no set formulas for how to change your life. In fact, I encourage all readers to challenge, disagree, and ultimately, come up with their own views and philosophies about the topics covered.

- **It is not a "health" book**, although at its basic level it is a book on how to cope with and minimize the stress in your life.

- **It is not a "philosophy" book,** but I do share my philosophies in many different areas and I ask readers to think about and write down their own philosophies while reading the book.

- **It is not a "religion" book**, although there are numerous references to a "Supreme Power" or "Supreme Being." My own background and upbringing is Southern Baptist, so my life experiences and observations come from that realm. Each reader must experience this book through the lens of his or her own spiritual senses. Those readers that do not relate to the spiritual aspects of living can simply adapt the lessons here to their own experience and beliefs. There is no right or wrong way to experience this book.

- **This book is a conversational essay.** I do not ask readers to accept everything I say here, but just to listen and evaluate. Every reader will take away a different set of lessons from this material. I wish I could simply sit down and talk to each reader individually, as I have done with my family, my children, my students, friends and colleagues. The next best thing is writing it all down for all to read on your own. I would like for this to be a reference book- something you refer to again and again over the years.

Life is not a destination, but an endless journey. Enjoy the ride to infinite processing.

How to use this book

This is a book that helps you look at where you are (how your life is going) and make some changes if you need to do that. It's not a "Bible" or anything etched in stone, but it gives you an idea of how to explore the various aspects of your life. It lets you know where you can go: family, community, church, school, and on the job. There are always people out there who can help you move up to the next level. My philosophy of life is what I call "infinite processing." You will never get there, but pleasure is in the journey. This is an eternal journey. You never cease to exist. Sometimes we get out of balance and our psyche has a way of letting us know what the problem is. Sometimes it's obvious: if you don't feel good, it's probably physical. If you are having trouble with money, you know it's financial. There are problems on the same level that are not as obvious; all you know is that something is just not quite right. So what do you do? That's where this book can help. Its purpose is to make you aware.

First, you want to try and identify the area of the problem: is it a problem with relationship? Is it one of spirituality? Once you've identified it, you need to make sure you are defining it correctly. The empirical meaning, or how it's described, is in the dictionary. Describing it is the first thing to learn. Then you have to figure out what you interpret from it. Also try to figure out what others interpret from it. Then you'll know you are talking about the same thing, or you can tweak the meaning such that you can agree. Next, explore how you feel about it: what are your values about these things? How do they affect you in your day-to-day living? That is your philosophy. Once you understand your own philosophy, then you can better understand the situation and how to deal with it. This book helps you through that process.

For each of the "real daily dozen" (Chapters 2-13), I have included the real definition according to *Webster's Dictionary*, and I've also talked about my own philosophy. Many people don't even know that they have a philosophy. The fact is, they just don't know that it exists. A philosophy always exists. Once we realize that everybody doesn't have the same definition and philosophy, that helps explain some of the problems we have with other people. When you talk to people, you have to first see how they define the issues and whether you define them that same way. Then if you are going to have interactions or relationships, you have to come to some type of agreement as to how you both are going to define them, although they both might not be defined the same way in different areas. Although I don't think there is a specific hierarchy to the various aspects of our lives, I do think spiritual, physical, and financial issues are probably more important than others. If your spiritual life is in order, you're physically fit and financially sound, then you can more easily deal with the other aspects of your life. These three are the linchpins of the whole thing. Although they are all important, if you can take control of these three, then you can fine-tune the others. If one aspect of your life is way out of kilter, it can affect the rest of your life.

    What I'm trying to do here is not only get you to look at yourself, but to look at your family, your job, your community, your country, and the whole world from the same definitions and the same philosophies. This is because if we were defining something differently (if I think I'm defining spirituality one way and you're defining it another way) then we're not really talking about the same thing. If I believe one thing and you believe something else, and the people in Greensboro, North Carolina believe something different from what we believe, I still need to know what they are thinking. I interact with them, in order for me to understand where there coming from and use the same language they use, I've got to understand their views and be able to resolve differences between us. I can do that by changing my views, convincing them to change theirs, or maybe coming up with some kind of compromise in which we take the best of both views. I'm not for creating problems for people, but I won't have certain things forced on me. How you react to people and things depends on your independence, and in a capitalistic society, independence usually means how much money you have and whether you are able to live without the support of those other people. If you're not able to live without support, then you have to be pragmatic at times. Certain financial restraints will keep people from doing certain things. I'm not trying to put anyone into a situation where they have to damage relationships or put their job or financial situation at risk just because they have a certain philosophy about something. You have to be able to look at the situation and know when you should do or say certain things. Ultimately, if you are going to be healthy, you will have to resolve those situations as best you can.

None of this is to be forced. None of this do you have to do. Readers will probably find that out of my "real daily dozen," they might have some other aspects they break down differently from the way I break them down. If you feel good with that, then break it out your way. You don't have to limit them to 12 and you can combine some of them. It's just that these areas exist, and recognizing this makes life more meaningful. It gives you a chance to keep on top of things that make your life pleasant and to deal with things that don't. I encourage readers to use this book as a way to look back over their lives to see where they are, to see where they want to go, and what philosophies they have. Are you defining things the right way? Is this really what you thought it meant? This book is just a guide to help you through that process. Some readers may want to read the book straight through while some others might choose to skip around, depending on the particular area they need help. Any way you choose to use the book is fine. After you finish reading it the first time, consider it to be a reference book and pull it out when new problems arise or when you think you need some extra help evaluating where you are. After all, the process of learning and growing never ends. Each of the "real daily dozen" has been researched and widely discussed in library books. Check them out, read them, and use them as resource lessons. This book is not a dissertation on the parameters, but as a guide to get you to the places you can go to get deeper meanings.

HARVEY D. HEARTLEY, SR.

DAILY/WEEKLY ACTIVITY SCHEDULE

Of _____ Week

Time	Monday	Tuesday	Wednesday	Thursday	Friday	Saturday	Sunday	Time
6:00	GET	UP	EVERY	DAY	AT	SAME	TIME	6:00
6:30								6:30
7:00								7:00
7:30								7:30
8:00								8:00
8:30								8:30
9:00								9:00
9:30								9:30
10:00								10:00
10:30								10:30
11:00								11:00
11:30								11:30
12:00								12:00
12:30								12:30
1:00								1:00
1:30								1:30
2:00								2:00
2:30								2:30
3:00								3:00
3:30								3:30
4:00								4:00
4:30								4:30
5:00	WORK	DAY	USUALLY	ENDS		BETWEEN	5&6	5:00
5:30							PM	5:30
6:00								6:00
6:30								6:30
7:00								7:00
7:30								7:30
8:00								8:00
8:30								8:30
9:00								9:00
9:30								9:30
10:00	GO	TO	BED		BETWEEN	10&11	PM	10:00
10:30								10:30

YOUR PERSONAL BEHAVIOR MAP TO SELF-FULFILLMENT

A Do-It-Yourself Fitness Program

	First Month	Second Month	Third Month
Warm-Up	15 min. jog	15 min. job	15 min. jog
Stretching	10 min. upper body	10 min. upper body	10 min. upper body
	10 min. lower body	10 min. lower body	10 min. lower body
Work-Out	5 push-ups	15 push-ups	30 push-ups
	25 crunches	35 crunches	50 crunches
	20 arm curls	30 arm curls	45 arm curls
	5 pull-ups	15 pull-ups	30 pull-ups
	20 leg curls	40 leg curls	50 leg curls
	10 squats	40 leg extensions	50 leg extensions
	1-mile run	20 squats	35 squats
Cool-down	15 min. jog	15 min. jog	15 min. jog
	5 min. walk	5 min. walk	5 min. walk
Stretching	10 min. upper body	10 min. upper body	10 min. upper body
	10 min. lower body	10 min. lower body	10 min. lower body

HARVEY D. HEARTLEY, SR.

Chapter 1

BASIC GUIDELINES FOR LIFE

This book reflects my philosophy on life – my views on how to live a fulfilling, happy and meaningful life. Many people don't think they have a philosophy – of life or anything else. I didn't give it any thought when I was a young man until I had an experience that made me stop and reevaluate things. When I first started coaching basketball, I had a job in a small, rural town. I thought I was coaching, but I was really just having fun. I coached both men and women, and I found myself playing along with them. I was spending a lot of time with them, but when we got ready to play, I found out that my players were not prepared to compete. That was a "wake –up call" for me. I realized that I had to organize practices and myself because there were basic things that the players needed to know. I got a book on the administration and supervision of physical education and athletics, and it said that before you start anything you have to have a philosophy of the sport. So I sat down and read some more books about the philosophies of most of the great basketball coaches, and I wrote out my own philosophy. I had learned self-discipline from my mother, who trained me to help her in many areas of our lives while my father was away in World War II. That same discipline helped me to organize my thoughts and prepare my team to play real basketball in a competitive way. From that lesson, I began to look at other areas of my life and realize that I needed a philosophy for each major element. Over the years, I've learned many lessons and I've refined my philosophies about many things, but I have never stopped believing in the importance of having a philosophy on different things and living by it. That's the ultimate lesson of this book. Whatever your philosophy may be, recognize it and live by it. If you don't have one, now is the time to take aim, think, and form one.

Basic guidelines for life

There are certain points that I make throughout this book, and I thought it would be helpful to summarize them up front. They are basic guidelines for life. Take a look at them here, because you will see them again, and again, in this book.

Infinite processing

We are all students of life for life. Learning and growing never end. Life is a process, and you can process to any level that you are willing to work to. There are no limits except the limits that we put on ourselves. I call this "infinite processing," and it's an important concept to keep in mind. Remembering that you're always learning will make you handle situations differently. It will make you think about what life lessons are teaching you at the moment. It will keep you constantly inquisitive and open to new thoughts and ideas. It will also make you a more interesting person to others. Most important of all, it will enable you to enjoy life to its fullest, because learning and growing is more fun than stagnating.

ICE (Intergenerational Collaborative "EnTergy")

This book is for all age groups and all generations. Throughout it, you will see how one generation can help another one and the importance of having all generations working together. I believe the most important way to help young people develop into the productive, contributing adults we want them to be is to enlist the help of their elders. Young people watch their elders and how they act or react based on what they see. By having parents, family members and grandparents of young people involved in their development (sharing their goals and participating with them in growth activities) we can accomplish a lot. Not only will young people feel the support of their families and their communities, the adults will feel more involved in the life of their children and will grow and learn along with them. When everyone is having fun together, great things can happen. You will see throughout this book how I look across generations to solve the problems. This is the ICE concept: ICE stands for "Intergenerational Collaborative EnTergy" (the T stands for "team"). It denotes TEAM ENERGY: everybody working together to accomplish team-oriented goals.

The paradox of life

Life is a paradox. Regardless of how well we plan, there will always be things that throw our plans out of kilter. Throughout our lives, we encounter instances when things just don't make sense. We naturally look for the logical, "right" answer to life questions, but there often isn't just one. The reason is that all of life itself is a paradox. Something can be both right and wrong depending on the view and/or the situation. Things can be different than they seem. In this lesson, we need to learn to be comfortable with that. Life is surprising and paradoxical. Get used to it. It keeps things interesting. It's not always either/or. It could be either/or/and.

30-day plan

Habits can be learned and broken in approximately 21 days. if there's something in your life you'd like to change, give it 30 days. Make the change and stick with them for a month. You'd be amazed of how much change can happen in a short period of time. I learned this many years ago, and I taught hundreds of students how to make a 30-day plan. It's something you will read about in the chapters of this book. Try it!

Get rid of the "thought police"

All through our lives, beginning when we were children, we were all sort of brainwashed about what we can and can't think, what we can and can't believe. It's a subtle thing; we're often not even aware of those monitors in our heads telling us what thoughts are off limits (which ones are not allowed). I was fortunate as a child to have parents and grandparents who encouraged me to challenge and question things. Even when I went way beyond what they believed, they didn't tell me what to think and what not to think. That is a valuable lesson that I want to pass on to the readers of this book. When you let the thought police censor what you think, you cheat yourself out of drawing your own conclusions - thinking for yourself. Whenever you sense that your thoughts are being influenced by the thought police , get rid of it, and let your thoughts run free. Only you know what's right for you based on your own philosophies of life.

A quick-look reference for time management to help gain control of your life

Post on your refrigerator door:

Time is one measure of life. Time wasted is life wasted. Time saved is life saved. Effective use of time, like effective use of money, is one way to find more enjoyment more success from our daily living. Each of us has at his or her command the same amount of time for each week- -exactly 168 hours; no more no less. Thus it is not the amount of time, but what you do with your time that counts most.

    The secret of more effective use of time and greater enjoyment of living lies in organizing and planning. Each person will, of course, plan his or her own 168 hours to harmonize with his or her unique requirements, inclinations and interests. But there can be no doubt that wise planning for the use of your time will provide more time for those things you are interested in doing. Each thirty minutes saved through planning is time that can be used to make life richer and better. Time planning is no major formula. Its value depends upon study, thought and effort. The plan suggested here should be a valuable asset to anyone who has the self-discipline to carry it though. To make it to work for you, however, you cannot give up and quit after a half-hearted initial effort.

Some wellness tips

1. Avoid cigarette smoking and all tobacco products.
2. Avoid drinking alcoholic beverages or drink no more than one or 2 drinks a day.
3. Eat a variety of foods each day, especially quantities of fruits, vegetables, whole grain breads, cereals and lean meats.
4. Limit the amount of fats, salts, spices and sugars.
5. Drink at least 8 glasses of water.
6. Maintain a desired weight; be neither underweight nor overweight.
7. Follow your designated fitness program (30-60 minutes daily or at least 4 times per week).
8. Have a worthy use of your leisure time. Participate in family and community activities often.
9. Limit your prescription drug intake to that prescribed by your doctor.
10. Do not use illicit drugs of any kind.
11. Always wear your seat belt and make sure others in the car do, also.
12. Get 8 hours of sleep a night.

Educational needs

Listed below are the primary skills one should possess to function successfully in any society. These skills should be mastered by the time one finishes high school and should be taught in all schools.

1. Reading, writing and arithmetic.
2. Vocational education or career education (job).
3. Common sense.
4. An appreciation of different cultures: yours and others.
5. Getting along with others.
6. Self-reliance, self-discipline.
7. A contributing citizen.
8. Self-esteem.
9. A healthy lifestyle.
10. Moral and ethical character.
11. An appreciation for art, literature and nature.
12. Being all you can be.
13. Spiritual awareness.

THE <u>REAL</u> DAILY DOZEN: LIFE'S TWELVE DEVELOPMENTAL TASKS (SPEMPP-FAR-SIS)

HARVEY D. HEARTLEY, SR.

Chapter 2

ATTITUDE

What are we talking about?

Webster's Dictionary defines attitude as "A mental feeling or position with regard to the fact or a particular situation." Often we do not have to say a word. People can look at the way you look, the way your head is dropping, the way you are walking, and the expression that you wear on your face. People really won't like to be around you if you have a bad attitude. Notice the little happy face that made someone millions of dollars. All they did was use some imagination. They drew a little funny face and put a little smile on it, and people everywhere bought it and wore it because everybody wants to be liked. And you'll be liked if you have a good attitude. I have a favorite saying: "Attitude determines altitude," which means that the attitude you bring to the situation generally determines how far you are going to go. I think history will bear out the fact that most of the people who have been successful and made good managers weren't the brainiest people in the world or the richest people in the world, but they were people who got along with others and were able to use a good attitude to get different groups of people together, organized, and moving on to the next level.

Same talent; different attitudes

I often think about two very successful basketball coaches I studied religiously, both brilliant with completely different coaching styles. One has an abrasive attitude: he engenders fear in others. The other commands respect. There's a thin line between fear and respect. I think you should respect people, but I don't think you should fear them. In the armed services, you have to fear because on the battlefield if you've got to take a hill, you can't have a democratic discussion about it. You have to follow orders. That's a very good approach if you are going to be a general. When you are dealing in public service where you can't order people around, you need a different type of attitude to get people to work with you. The former coach I referred to is on a collision course with disaster because of his attitude. It is only a matter of time before he self-destructs.

Start your day off right

Always have a positive mental attitude (I call it "PMA"). When I get up in the morning to go into the bathroom to brush my teeth, I look in the mirror above the sink and I say, "Every day, in every way, I am getting better and better and better." I repeat that three times as I look at myself in the mirror. If you are having trouble looking at the man or woman in the mirror, then some aspect of your life is messed up. You might not know what it is, but if you didn't like what you saw in the mirror and you are having problems when you are looking at yourself, then chances are your life elements are out of balance. You want to be able to say, " Every day in every way, I am getting better and better and better." Say it with a smile on your face and believe it. That starts the day off right. Once you've done that, you always want to think about what happened yesterday and what you are going to do today that's going to make you have a good day. You are going to iron out those things that you messed up yesterday, if possible. If you hurt somebody's feelings or did something you shouldn't have, you need to call that person or see them and say, "I made a mistake. I was a little tired or a little irritable," and set it straight. They may or may not accept your apology, but you get it off your chest. You can move on from there. You don't have to worry every time you see them crossing the street. You get it cleared out, and then you move on. If they choose to hold on to it, that's their problem, but you get rid of it.

Most people don't start the day the way I described. They don't think about what they did yesterday. For one thing, most people are going to a job they don't want to go to. That makes it hard to maintain a positive mental attitude. Parents and grandparents need to start their kids off right, so that they'll enjoy starting every day. You want them to be so excited that they can't wait to get up in the morning to go to school, because school is going to be enjoyable. You tell them it's going to be fine; it's going to be fun, and they are shaping themselves to be whatever they want to be. Whatever they tell you they want to be, you never tell them they can't be that. When a person first starts reading this book and living like this, there's a good chance you are not going to feel as good as you did before. That's what happens when we do a self- examination. This is an x-ray book, and if you do this right, you won't be able to hide from yourself.

The lesson of "MacBasketball"

My basketball coach in college was named John McLendon. He was a great man and I loved him like a father. He was truly a brilliant man. Coach used to make us play a game called "MacBasketball." He coined that name for a 3-on-3, full court game that he invented. It had to be played from baseline to baseline, and for defense, you always had to be 1 arm away from your man. You had to guard your player with no help. Coach talked about 4 degrees of defense.

You had to get the ball across the court in 5 seconds, which meant that there was no rest. If you rested, the other team got a point. The team that lost had to stay up until they were just about to drop. He would put a guard on a guard, a forward on a forward, and a center on a center. He would start with the first team and then go to the second team and the third. Out there on the floor, everybody got to see who were the best players. It was nose-to-nose. I can tell you that once fatigue sets in and you lose it, it is not any fun. "That's the price you pay for losing," according to the coach. It was just a game; Coach Mac would just smile. He wouldn't say a thing, but everybody knew. It was the x-ray game because it let everybody in the gym know whether you could play or not. Fatigue makes cowards of one of us all. That's where derived my philosophy in basketball: "90/40 smoke and smother." The basketball court is 94 feet long, the games last about 40 minutes, and during the whole time, my team was expected to keep moving (smoking) and smother the opposing team. Never let up for a minute! Our philosophy was that if we were in 10 points within the last 6 minutes of the game, we were going to beat the other team.

We were going to beat them on condition alone, because we were going to be all over them and they wouldn't be able to jump or run, pass or shoot. We use to beat teams unmercifully, and we wouldn't even be tired at the end of the game. If we were on the road, we'd play another game after that, just among ourselves. That was the kind of shape we were in. We ran 3½ miles every morning before practice, and then we'd run 3½ miles in the evening. Then we would run the steps. We were in terrific shape. That's why I played in high school and in college, and I coached all my teams that way. Everybody knew when we came in, and we packed gyms in high schools and colleges. People came from miles around because it was so exciting. It was non-stop.

We called it playing "Simon Pure," which was reference from my childhood in Clayton, North Carolina. When I was a child, liquor was not available commercially in the community where I lived, but there was a lot of "white liquor" (homemade) around. This stuff had no proof on it. It was so strong, when you drank it, it almost came out of your ears and nose. The best from miles around was made by a man named Simon. People began to refer to things as "Simon Pure" if they had no imperfections. That's the way our basketball was – Simon Pure. I still teach youngsters the same way. Today, if I conduct a basketball clinic on defense, I'll say, "This is Coach McLeadon's 4 degrees of defenses," and then I will take 3 people or 4 people out on the court and show them. These days, instead of calling that kind of game " Simon Pure," your likely to hear the phrase, " No shame in my game."

A good attitude starts with how you treat your family

When you get up in the morning, make sure you greet everybody in the family with a smile and encourage them to have a good day. Ask them how their day is going so far, and tell them you hope everything is going to be all right. Ask if there's any way you can help them. If you do this, then everybody should leave the house in a pretty good frame of mind. If not, you can talk about it, either right then or later when there is time. Say, "When we come home this evening, we need to sit down and toss this thing around and see what we can do to help the situation." I tried to do that with my own children, so I didn't have a lot of problems that did not surface with them. When something came up, they said, "Hey Daddy, I think you and I need to talk about some things." So we'd sit down and talk. My wife would join us. Sometimes the girls would want to talk to her, then she would tell me either directly or indirectly if they didn't want me to know. But there was always an open dialogue, and it was to help everybody to be as pleasant as they could possibly be. I've always said, "Now don't bring me any gloom and doom."

Inspiration on the move

After you've you told the family goodbye in the

morning and you're headed to work or school, you want to listen to some inspirational, business or educational tapes in the car. There's a lot of road rage out there, so put on your happy face and positive thinking tapes, CDs, or .mp3 files, or some learning tapes, CDs, or .mp3 files. I have a library of just tapes. When some aspects of my life are not exactly how they ought to be, I just flip a tape in, and while I drive it will tell me what I need to know. There are tapes available for everything you can imagine – all aspects of your life. I have some meditation tapes that I put on at night and turn the lights off, and they just take me right on through whatever it is I want to do. So put on those positive tapes and smile at people on the freeway. Don't give them the finger or dirty looks. If they're honking and glaring at you, just smile and nod and let them think you're a dodo. Reacting any other way just might get you shot these days. Check your pride and show that positive attitude.

Attitude at work

Greet everybody on the job by saying, "Good morning! How are you? How's everything going?" with a little twinkle in your eye. Offer a word of encouragement and hum a little tune or something. Keep that same demeanor all day, regardless of whether you really want to jump up and hit somebody in the mouth, because you can't do that. It doesn't help. Pretty soon, people will want to be around you. They'll look to you to see what you are doing. If you are doing your job in a professional manner, they'll see that, and the boss will start inviting you to things. All the time you be thinking about where you want to go in the organization. Study those people that are immediately above you so you can please them first. Find out what they want – not what you want, but what they want – and see if you can make it happen. Once you've figured them out, then think about their bosses. Once your boss moves up, he or she has got to recommend somebody into his place. If you've been showing a nice attitude, being a company person and being helpful, then your boss will recommend that you move up. That's the way you move up the ladder without backstabbing and trying to make somebody else look bad. Never do that. Do your job and treat everybody else well.

There are many books, audiotapes, CDs, and .mp3s on corporate management and how to get ahead. I gave my son and daughter one on "How to become a CEO." There are 27 things they state as to what to do to become a CEO. So put that on in your car and listen to it on the way to work and do what it says.

Lastly, find a mentor. Find out what mentors do, and you do it too. That's called mirroring. Do the things that people you admire and want to be like do.

Bad attitude

What happens when you encounter people with

bad attitudes? The first thing you have to do is try to find out why they have a bad attitude. Is it just today? Is it periodically, or is it constantly? You owe it to them and yourself to pull them aside at some point, with a smile of course, and say, "You know, it seems like I get on your nerves, or there's something about me, something that I'm doing that seems to upset you. Would you mind telling me what it is?" That takes them off guard. Sometimes it's trivial, but usually there is some reason, and you might not be aware of it. Even when they recall it to you, you might not remember what it was, but then you might have to apologize. You have to be bigger than they are, and say, "Well, I really didn't know that. I was not aware. But I think you're a nice person and were here working together and I see you and you have to see me, so let's try to be pleasant to one another and not hurt one another. If I can help you, fine. Let me know. I'll be willing to help. I'm glad you told me. I hope you have a nice day." Then, move on. If they continue to have a bad attitude towards you, then just try to avoid them, because they have some problems.

The value of failure

When I was first coaching, I lost a heartbreaking game in Richmond, Virginia. I was younger at the time, about 37 years old, and I shouldn't have lost this game, but fate just got me. The kids did the opposite of the things I told them to do, not because they wanted to, but the pressure got to them. Then with 3 seconds left, a guy shot a ball that seemed to have no way of going in, but it hit up on top and fell in...and we lost the game. We didn't go to the tournament, even though we had worked so hard. I was really shaken because it looked like we were going to get a chance to go. Tom Harris, who was a legend in coaching at the time, saw it. He liked me because I was younger and bodacious, and he came over and dropped his arm on me. He said, "Yeah, you should have won this game. Fate works like that sometimes. Sometimes you can do all you should do, all the planning you want, and it doesn't work out. Providence just says 'Hey, it ain't going to happen.'" Then he said, "But let me tell you one thing. Always let defeat prepare you for your next success. I want you to remember that, write that down." I put that up on my wall. I wrote it down on a card and I put it up behind my desk. I've had some stinging defeats since then, but I think God was preparing for roles of leadership at a later point in time. He wanted to let me know how it felt and to teach me how to make the most of it.

Unfairness

In addition to failures, I've had people make questionable decisions on more than one occasion, and even sometimes more than once, on some occasions. I couldn't imagine how in the world adult, educated people do the things that they did.

It showed me that when you are out there dealing with the public – and these were the elite of the elite – they would do all manner of things to win (things I never would do). In sports, you are playing to see who has prepared the best, and want everything fair because that's what the rules say. Then to see people who are in the education field, of all the fields, it hurts me that they did things they shouldn't have done. There was a voice that said to me, "I'm preparing you for some things down the road, so you will be able to understand them." In the long run, it never really bothered me. The funny thing is that the crowds, people from both sides always said, "Man, you won that game. You won that tournament. They just took it from you!" Those things happen, and over the years I've learned that as long as I have a positive mental attitude and do the best I can, the unfairness does not really bother me. I'm able to get over it and get ready for the next thing. Still, it's hard to explain to kids, "Keep your head up! We know that people cheated you, and that happens."

Leaders and attitude

A positive attitude is essential for a leader who needs to be able to work with other people and encourage them to have positive outlooks, too. When you see people with attitudes that are not complimentary to their success, you need to let them know in a subtle way that their problems are probably due to attitude more than anything else.

Most people are skilled at what they do (reasonably competent) but it's their attitudes and little idiosyncrasies that keep them from rising above the pettiness. Attitude permeates everything! I've worked with organizations and served on numerous committees, and the biggest problem getting people to cooperate is their negative attitudes. When it comes to leadership, I believe in "bottoms up, participatory, democratic leadership." I call it " BUPDL."

This approach to leadership applies within the family as well as the job. In most instances, the father is the leader in the household. It's not that he knows more than the mother, but if you go back to the natural order of things, the reason the man became the head of the household is because the wife was going to get pregnant. In an agrarian society, when she was pregnant and had kids, he had to be the person to go out to get things. It didn't mean he was smarter, it didn't mean he was a better leader. It meant at some point in some time, the woman was going to be incapacitated, and in order for the household to keep going, society set it up that the man was head of the household in most instances. Both parents have responsibilities in a household, and if there is a conflict, they need to resolve it objectively. Don't let your egos get the best of you. Often a man doesn't want to go along with something because it's the woman's idea, and women often have the same attitude towards men. We're all supposed to be on the same team. We're supposed to take the best idea, agree on it jointly, and do it. You can never know up front who has the best idea because consequences determine whether it's a good choice or not. There are going to be consequences, so you just decide which you think is best and deal with it. If it turns out to be a bad idea, then you just say, "Whoops, that was wrong," without attacking people.

Parents really should set positive attitude atmosphere. There are times when I think either father or the mother should bring everybody together and sit down and say, "This family is getting dysfunctional and I think we need to address some things here." That approach applies to organizations beyond family, too. The leader should bring everybody together. The basic unit of society is the family. If you can straighten up the families, everything else will be straightened up. Attitude starts first with you – how do you feel about yourself? Then it goes to your family. Then it goes to people that you don't even know on the highway. Then it goes to the job. Then it goes to organizations. In all of those instances, somebody had to take the lead to be able to see and say some things are out of whack. When you call a meeting, you have points listed. You have to put them in order of importance – a hierarchy of dysfunctionality. Then you address them by getting everyone's input. You reach a consensus about what to do to resolve watch issue. Then you say, "We've had a good meeting." Everybody has participated.

If a family runs pretty smoothly, then when the children grow up and leave usually they'll take those same traits wherever they go. When I was a boy, we used to have family meetings where we would sit around the table and discuss things. Everybody had his say. Everybody. I think that came about because we used to have family Thanksgiving dinners and Christmas dinners and we would talk about things – family things. It has always been an open family. There have always been teachers in my life – teachers, preachers and deacons.

Personal accountability

My basic premise is that it's up to the individual to make something out of his or her life. Regardless of your family background, it's up to you. Don't come telling me your troubles – that you were poor, or you didn't have a father, or whatever. I hear you, and I'm sorry you didn't have all the advantages, but we are here now. What are we going to do now? What are you going to do today? What are you going to do tomorrow? What's your plan? How do you see yourself? You're responsible for you.

I have never treated little kids as little kids. Somebody said, "That's why they love you, because you always let them talk." They say, "Little kids and old folks just love you," because I take time for them. I have a nice personality, and I smile with them, and if you think that won't work just smile at a kid and nod your head at him. He'll come over and play with you. Youngsters have something on their mind, too. There are no blank minds. It might not be something that their cognitive equipment can handle yet, but there's something on their minds. Ask them, "What is it you want to talk about?" Their thoughts and solutions might not be realistic or even lucid yet, but the thinking is there, and eventually at some time it's going to mature and make sense. The good parent or mentor is able to stay ahead of the curve and can anticipate. What the next question will be. Then when it comes, you're prepared with some good answers.

A daily routine

When you go to bed at night, give yourself a little time – I usually take 30 minutes – and just relax and think about the day. Praise whatever powers there are for whatever happened that day, the good and the bad. Then think about what you want to do the next day to have another good day. Then sleep well. Go to bed early and get up early. Be discriminating in what you watch on TV. Watch your time, because in my daily activity schedule, there's a 6 o' clock "get up" time, and a then 11 o' clock "go to bed" time. In those hours in between, you're either going to be doing something productive or you're going to be asleep.

Anger

I was always supervised and disciplined from an early age. When things came up, I saw how other people handled those issues. My father was an easygoing man. My uncle was a deacon. My grandfather was a deacon. My great uncle was a preacher. They were lovely people. I saw how they handled things. I didn't see any uncontrolled anger when I was growing up. Even in athletics, which is a highly passionate endeavor, I've lost championships about which I felt outrage. But I never cursed the officials out. There's a one-liner that says it all for me: "If you lose your head, your _ _ _ is sure to follow."

There have been some real hot situations, but usually in those instances, you have to walk away. You have to realize where you're going and what you're doing because once you say something that hurts somebody, that's a wound that never heals. I always try to walk away. Well, I try not to let it get to that point. If I see it going that way, I'll just say, "Well, let's just table this for now, and come back to it later." Usually, that will do it.

Of course, you don't want to put yourself into situations where there is ongoing tension. You don't want to have a job were you don't like the people you work with or you don't like the boss. It's heck all day. Hopefully, by getting in touch with the various aspects of your life, you will be able to say in that kind of situation, "You know, this is not really working out. You have your thoughts about what a relationship should be and I have mine. It looks like they've gone in different directions. We're just making each other miserable, I'm going to do you a favor. I'm going to leave. I'm not going to ask you to leave. We'll work out the terms. You know I don't have anything against you, but this is causing me mental anguish and I can't live my life like this, so I'm out of here." Then have somewhere to go and something to do. Then, just move on with your life.

Don't let negative things get you down

Former NBA star Magic Johnson spoke to a group of our students shortly after he learned that he had AIDS. We had an AIDS awareness rally at Memorial Auditorium, and he came to St. Augustine's College and spoke. I picked him up at the airport. He said, "Well, you know, yeah, I've got this disease. But I've just got to keep on stepping." With his smile and everything, the students really learned the power of positive thinking. Memorial Auditorium was packed. I sort of picked that up from Magic. Regardless of the situation, you've got to keep on stepping.

At the end of this chapter and each succeeding chapter, there will be a few things for you to do in order to have some type of measurable evaluation to guide you in your self-development process.

Please buy yourself a spiral notebook with at least 100 pages for confidential notes. After each chapter, write out your philosophy, feelings, and findings. Do not share them with anyone at any time. When you finish, stud it and update it.

Some things to do

1. On a scale of 1 – 10 (1 – lowest, 10 highest), how would you rate your attitude at:

   A. Home
   B. Work
   C. Place of worship
   D. Community participation?

2. How do you think your spouse or significant other rates your attitude?
3. How do you think your boss rates your attitude? Your co-workers?
4. How do you think your children rate your attitude?
5. Write down how you can improve your attitude in all the aforementioned areas.
6. Go to the library. Talk with the librarians. Get on-line. Do research.
7. Find a good coach.
8. Do what you want to do.

HARVEY D. HEARTLEY, SR.

Chapter Three

RELATIONSHIPS

What are they?

Webster's Dictionary refers to a relationship as: "The state of being related or interrelated; the state of being mutually interested or involved." My own personal definition is that relationships are the day-to-day involvement that one has with other individuals, groups or a community. My philosophy on relationships is that all relationships should be workable, so that both parties are the better off by having the relationship than they would be if it didn't exist. It's what I call a win-win situation.

Balance in relationships

On any given day, you might not feel that way. Feelings will come and go within a relationship until the parties have settled into their comfortable roles. Relationships need to be defined along with what it is that you actually want to receive out of the relationship. Most of the time, people want relationships to be skewed in their favor. That's human nature. At the same time, you don't want to take advantage of other people such that you get more than you take. Most relationships aren't 50/50, but over time there should be a balance that you both can live with.

You should never compromise your integrity in a relationship because, over the long run, the relationship will break down and you will find yourself expressing a lot of anger and rage at some point in the future. Nor should you put anyone else in a situation where they'll have to compromise their own integrity. You have to always control your ego because it will get you into a really big trap. The Bible says, *"Pride goeth before destruction, and a haughty spirit before stumbling."* (Proverbs 16:18) I equate the two – pride and ego – and consider how we're going to look in the eyes of other people. Sometimes you will do things that will be detrimental to you and the relationship. You've got to be very, very careful that you don't fall into what I call the ego trap, or the integrity trap. You've got to be able to look at yourself in the morning, and you don't want to look in the mirror and not like that person that you see. If that happens, you're going to be crushed from the inside.

All relationships should make us better people and should help us on our infinite processing route. If they don't, they need to be restructured, if possible.

Family relationships

The first relationship anyone experiences is with the family. You're born into that relationship; you have no choice. When you are young, you should feel wanted and loved, and you should be taught those traits that you need to be a good family member. It's up to our parents to make sure that the relationships are good between parent and child and also among siblings. Then you have extended family: the grandparents, uncle, aunts, cousins, etc. Then you move from there to your neighbors and your community. Then you go to your church or your faith organization, your schools, and ultimately your job or profession. All of these relationships should enrich your life and should also make the other person or organization better.

Always contribute as much as you can in a relationship without feeling that you're being taken advantage of. Some people can give more than others. Some people are just genetically geared to be able to give more than others. Some people are takers; others are givers. I'm not saying one is better than the other, but you need to know which one you are; and you need to try to give as much as you receive.

I was conditioned to be a giver. I was brought up in an unusual situation, in that there was a war going on. My father was fighting in the World War II, and I was with my mother. We were both very young, and I had to do the things that needed to be done. I had to assume a role of significant responsibility and I just figured that was normal. I didn't question it because I didn't know anything else, because my father was not there. Then when my brothers were born, I helped take care of them, because they wanted me to, and I didn't have any problem with that. Like many first children, I've been very responsible all my life. I had no problem with it, plus I always had something to give. When I was going to school, the teachers selected the kids that understood what they were doing to help the kids who didn't understand. Nobody had any problems with that. If you didn't understand, you asked somebody. I didn't know about everything, but I could ask someone else. We were always sharing and I think that's the way that it should be.

Teaching and learning relationships

When I started teaching, I quickly found that there are five levels of students: those who are way out there, those who are not too far out there, those who are average, those who are below average, and those who probably shouldn't even be in the class. I call those five the A, B, C, D and F groups. Students don't always stay in the same group they start in depending upon their comprehension, but you start the work as a team at an early age. Those who understand the subject become the teachers of those who don't. As the teacher, I set the tone by letting them know that nobody has a cap on all the knowledge. Everybody brings something to the table, so what we're going to do is work together as a team of 5 people. We're going to tackle this problem in the group. Then I would let the groups compete against each other. After some time, they came to love that because everybody loves competition. You earned some extra bonus points if your group won, and then we would switch the groups around. We didn't keep them the same. It was just a marvelous way to teach and to learn. There was a lot of energy in the room.

 I think work relationships should be the same way. On the job, you should have managers who are good at the job help the people who are not. The introduction of the "at will" environment in corporate America has been detrimental to on-the-job relationships. Now if I help you, you're going to get the job, and they'll fire me. In corporations, we need to let everybody know that they are valued and that, as long as the numbers are as they should be, there will be no firing or layoffs. We can't afford to be tight-fisted with compensation. The way to maintain this kind of environment is to have such an effective organization that you out-produce the competition, and everybody shares in the pie. If, based on business results, the pie is getting smaller, then we try to figure out how we can make it bigger again. This is the type of relationship I like to be in, whether it's at home, in church, on a team, or whatever.

Family reunions

We also had family reunions as big affairs of 80-100 to a hundred people. We always had a Christmas dinner in the immediate family. We sort of kept up that tradition since I was a kid, and as of the time I am writing this, I'm 65 years old. One of the things I remember most fondly was the fact that my grandparents made wine. At Christmas, everybody could drink wine. It was a small demitasse cup given to the entire family, but that was our family wine. Not only did she make the best wine in the world, but she also made a fruit cake. She started that real early in the season, and she poured wine over it. It was just a great time. We bought Christmas presents for everybody.

Learning about positive caring relationships starts with family, and then it goes into schools. It's up to the principal to set the tone in every school so each kid knows that he or she's welcomed there and the teacher knows that they're to do a job and help these youngsters to become all they can become. Teachers need to help these students understand they are a school family. Both teachers and students should make each other believe that they are going to have the best school, bar none, wherever it is.

When I was growing up, the teacher played with us. We played basketball, volleyball, softball and competed. We just had a good time. The teachers we knew were really interested in us as individuals. They'd whip our butt just as quick as they would smile at us. They weren't whipping us because they didn't like us, and it wasn't brutality or abuse. They did it because they cared. These days, unfortunately, teaching is becoming just a job.

Everybody needs to work (it's a good solution for poverty, boredom, and low self-esteem), and relationships in the community are important parts of our lives. In the work environment, there should be an esprit de corps that exists all the way from top to bottom. The same spirit that is engendered in the family should apply to the work community. One of the biggest reasons why we can produce so much in America is because we give a certain amount of democratic freedom to workers. I think people definitely should be rewarded. Relationships are better when there are plenty of resources available for everybody. That way, no one can think that if they achieve they will be putting someone else at a disadvantage. We need to foster the belief that we all are going to achieve. Although it might not be at the same level, we're going to do everything we can to help each other.

Male/female relationships

There's a lot written and talked about these days concerning the antagonistic relationships between men and women: they don't understand each other; they speak different languages, etc. that has been bought about by the fact that everybody now can be independent, based on their wishes, and their ability to go out and earn on their own. Now that women have the opportunity to earn as much as men (almost, anyway) there is some balance and equality in male/female relationships. There may also be more tension because of this. Women have their own ideas, and their work skills are just as good as men's, which, in some instances, makes men feel threatened. I like to look at it from an individual standpoint: biologically we're different, but from the standpoint of entering into a relationship, we've both got to bring something to the table. It was my objective to bring up both my sons and my daughters pretty much the same. Although I realized there are biological differences, they all had chores to do and we rotated those chores so that there was no such thing as a "girl's job" or a "boy's job." Everybody had to wash the dishes and everybody mowed the grass. If the girl's curfew was 12, then the boy's curfew was 12, too. When you raise children in a way that they can play all roles, they learn to have a greater appreciation for both genders. When they grow up, they don't suffer from old-fashioned gender stereotype thinking.

Relationships with our children

In entering into an intimate relationship, each of us needs to think carefully about the question of bringing children into the world. Before making a decision to have a child or run into the risk of having an unplanned child, we need to have thoughts of how we would take care of that person. In the classes I taught where we dealt with intimate relationships and sexuality, I did not let the females take only the female point of view. They had to be the male too; and the males had to think like the females. If you were a male, I made you approach the problem and defend the problem from the female point of view. Whoever won the debate won the debate. There were some interesting outcomes to this teaching approach. We found out that males had a male psyche about things, and female had a female psyche about things. In my college classes, most of the guys wanted to have their careers and they wanted their wives to stay home and take care of the children. Well, we found out that the females wanted to work, too. There was a fact that you couldn't get around: if you're going to have children, somebody is going to have to take care of them. Now who's going to do it? Are you going to be making a lot of money? What are the chores that you want to do? What are the chores that you don't want to do? We found out, over a period of years, that nobody really wanted to do the dirty work. The males didn't want to do it and neither did the females. They wanted to do the things that were glamorous. They did not want to stay home and take care of the children.

My own philosophy on childrearing

I believe that the first few years of your marriage should be spent planning the rest of your life together. You shouldn't have children until the wife or husband can stay at home with the children for the first 3 years. The first 3 years of the child's life are a critical development period, and I don't think it starts after a baby is born. Once a couple decides to have a child, I think the wife or husband should stop working, or he or she shouldn't go past the point where work is going to create stress. I think that those 3 years are the most important 3 years of a child's life, and both parents need to sacrifice to make sure the child's life start off on the right foot. I know this is a controversial position these days and, like everything else in this book, I offer it up for your consideration only. Each individual must make his or her own decisions about how to live their lives. However, in a marriage, a couple should discuss these subjects and reach a mutually agreeable decision on how to handle the responsibility of raising children. This obviously links to managing the financial aspect of your life, which is discussed in a later section. Your finances should be in shape where somebody can stay at home with the children for three years. This is an ideal situation, in my opinion. If both parents have to work, one should take on work that does not a take a lot of time away from the children. This is the period where the parents should try to gear their youngsters for life.

Before you have children, you have to develop a philosophy of parenting and having children. My definition of a parent is someone willing to take care of a person the rest of their life, if need be. We always assume that our children will be healthy and when they are 18 or 21, they will be grown up and on their own, but that does not always happen. If you bring children into the world you have to be able to support them if necessary for as long as they live. Many people don't think about that. If you have a kid that is ill equipped to deal with the world, then what are they going to do? When you get ready, you've have to first think, " This is my child for life."

Parenting is a relationship for life

If you are going to bring kids into the world, hopefully you'll chose a mate to complement what you gave them, insomuch as the children are going to have to live with the genes you give. You don't want to bring a child into the world who's at a disadvantage if you can avoid it. That kind of thinking is going to create some problems for some people. Some people will say they don't think it's right to consider such things. I'm just letting you know that could create a problem for the children, so don't be surprised. Don't say you didn't know.

This is the purpose of the relationship. There are many famous books on parenting, and you need to get a grasp of how to take care of and raise a baby before you actually have one. Biologically speaking, after the end of 4 years, a baby will have developed most of his or her personality traits. Then it's just a matter of training. I think the mother and father both work together to supplement whatever needs to be done. After that, you raise them together. I think primary that is the way nature prepared us to raise children. After the kids are older, if mother or father wants to go back to work and you're able to do it financially, he or she should go back to whatever he or she needs or wants to do. Give the kids the best training you can afford. Sacrifice!!

There's going to be strain on the intimate part of the marriage relationship when there's so much focus on raising the children. The couple needs to make sure and find time to be intimate with each other. They will both be busy during the day, so the time that they are going to have will be in the evenings or on weekends.

I was fortunate to have a job everybody enjoyed doing. We went to the ball game and other activities as a family. The kids went with us. Even when they were babies, we put them in pasteboard boxes and carried them with us, and the fans would hold them in the boxes. They were socialized that way. We never really had problems finding ways to spend time together. Later, we were able to put them in good kindergartens and our relationship didn't suffer. Neither did the kids suffer. Now, I realize it was an ideal situation.

The marriage relationship

Communication is very important for a couple to keep their marriage healthy. They need to sit down and discuss problems before they internalize them and then all of a sudden they erupt. Then one person says, "I didn't know that you felt that way." You need to air out all those problems that exist (not every day). If you see that habits are starting to form, you need to be able to sit down with your spouse and say, "I think we need to talk about this," not in order to accuse or blame, just to say. Ask questions like, "How do you feel we need to resolve this?" "This is how I feel. How do you feel?" If you love each other, you'll come to some pretty good conclusions. I think the best way to have a male/female relationship, if you want to have kids, is to be married. The reason for that is once you're married, you're making a commitment. Hopefully you're making a commitment for life, but it might not last for life. You need to make a relationship for as long as you think you might need it. If you want kids, you need to make it last a long time so the kids will not suffer. Marriage makes one take a commitment. It makes one think about things. It lets the public know what your thoughts are. Plus, it protect the children and particularly the mother, because you have a legal entity to make sure that the mother and children are financially taken care of in case things don't work out down the road. If your spouse says, " I don't think I like this anymore, and I think I'm going to leave," then you're left out there. It's best to have the relationship supported legally in terms of protecting your property rights. Some people like cohabitation; many people do it. It might be an OK lifestyle for the very rich or the very poor (in the former case, one may pay for whatever might come up at a later time, and in the latter, one doesn't have anything, so it really doesn't matter). For the majority of people, I think marriage is best.

If your marriage doesn't last

Over a period of years people change, situations change, and many relationships don't last. Nature does not create a union called marriage. Marriage is a creation of human beings. Biologically, at the end of four years, the giddy-like passion or fiery intimate relationship that exists between two people fades. This is because nature equips men to make sure that the species survived, to have many partners so that the genetic material would be spread around for improved species. Therefore, if one relationship did not produce offspring, then another one would. From the stand point of nature, the love relationship is going to be redefined over time. There are different types and degrees of love, and you cannot endure the type of physiological expressions that passion is going to put on you forever because the intensity is great and you would be unable to proceed upward in your relationship. If marriage doesn't last and there is a divorce, there should still be a type of relationship between the two people that is in best interest of the children. This is true, regardless of how or why the divorce might come about. It takes a pretty big person to get past hurt and anger, but you should have the interest of the other person and the children at heart.

Alternative lifestyles and relationships

Society has developed some norms and rules over time that work best for civilization in general. Things that work best for civilization and society are not always best for the individual. No one should stay in a relationship that is detrimental to his or her health: physical, mental or emotional. We don't really know what lifestyles are good for other people. We can only say what lifestyle is best for us. Although there are lifestyles that are outside the norm or are not what society would like them to be, they're not dangerous or threatening to the rest of the world. Relationships should not only be in best interest of all parties involved, but they should not be detrimental to other people. If a relationship meets that test, then why not be in it? It's simply a matter of choice. God did not give us answers; He gave us choices.

Some things to do

1. On a scale of 1 – 10 (1 – lowest, 10 highest), how would you rate your relationship with:

    A. Your spouse or significant other
    B. Your boss
    C. Your co-worker
    D. Your children
    E. Your family members
    F. People of different races

2. What relationships do you need to improve?
3. Write out your plans for improving your relationships.
4. Give a copy of this book to a community member that you think could use it. Discuss it with him or her over lunch. Invite him or her over for dinner.
5. Go to the library. Talk with librarians. Go online. Do research.
6. Find a good coach.
7. Do what you want to do.

CHAPTER 4

IMAGINATION

What is it?

Imagination is the basis of all creation, because it is the ability to think and fantasize without limits. *Webster's Dictionary* defines imagination as "The act of forming a mental image of something not present to senses, or previously known or experienced." My thoughts are everything that started with imagination. God had to have an imagination. Out of His imagination came thoughts, and out of these thoughts, He was able to create His thoughts through words, and then deeds. Creation usually start with a perception thought, then word or words, then deeds or actions, so I think of the imagination as the being part of the creative process. Thoughts bombard our minds all day. The brain is never vacant. There's always something on the mind.

According to research, between 40,000 to 80,000 thoughts come to our mind in the course of a 24-hour period. If you think about it, there's never any time when your mind is blank. There's always something up there, and it goes very fast. It's always happening, regardless of whatever else you're doing. I'm talking about imagination without limits, and imagination pervades all aspects of our lives. How can you imagine how healthy you can be? There are no limits! Try thinking and imagining without limits or boundaries. Through processes called creative visualization and verbal affirmations, you can literally create your future. If you can visual imagine or see where you want to go, and if you can tell yourself over and over how it's going to be, those are two ways in which you can do things. It's been proven that you can learn how to hit a golf ball better by sitting back and visualizing the perfect golf swing and how to do it. Verbal affirmation means that after you see yourself doing something, you say out loud what you've done, and you can see yourself actually doing it. Praise and congratulate yourself on the accomplishment. Be what you intend to be. Behave as if you already are.

How to turn random ideas into realities

Everything in this world was created. It all came from thought and imagination. So in order to tap into your imagination and let it work for you, you need to open your mind to all the thoughts running through it. Once these thoughts are bombarding your mind, imagination will run rampant. There will be some that will interest you more than others, and those that will cause you to pursue the next step: fantasizing. After you've imagined something, then fantasize about how far you can take it. You do this without imposing any limits on your imagination. The difference between imagination and fantasizing is a more active focusing in your mind about how big an idea could be. In the imagination phase, the idea just floats into your mind. I personally believe that all thoughts come from and go to a supernatural realm – a spiritual world. I think that everything that has ever been thought or will be thought is out there, and it's up to us to be able to tap into it and retrieve those thoughts. When I say you need to fantasize "without limits," I mean you catch yourself thinking that some things are not possible, or that it can't happen, you have to stop yourself. Open back up. Once you get through the fantasy phase, then you then about the possibilities. You introduce a little bit of reality to the pictures. What's possible is usually dictated by the availability of resources, including people. After you have explored the possibilities of an idea, you then focus on the probabilities. Then you establish some hypotheses, which are selected solutions that you can use at a particular point in time. After you assess the possibility of an idea, you'll find that you don't have all the resources you need. You don't have all the knowledge, you don't have all the people, etc. but within that imaginative thought, you have found something tangible that you want to do and you believe is possible and probable. Now you have moved to unlimited thought to pragmatic possibilities. Then you have to choose one or two of the possibilities that you think you can actually pull off to create whatever it is that you want to create.

Now here comes the challenge: you have to do the research. You have to find out what it is and what it isn't. After you research the literature and talk to experts, then you need to form an opinion as to think how it would work for you. This could involve either improving on something that already exists, or creating something that has never existed. Once you develop your information base, you will know where to go. At this stage you need to write your plan down in detail. You don't have to do this by yourself: you can get as many people involved with you as is necessary. You can form what I call an "enTergy," that is, the team based energy effort. If you consider corporations and venture capitalists, all of them started with an idea and imagination, and then they persuaded other people that their ideas were good. Henry Ford imagined a world with cars; scientists fantasized about television; Bill Gates and his colleagues imagined life with Microsoft software, etc. All of those ideas were elements of imagination first, and then became realities. Those visionaries had to get other people to believe (bankers, research people, engineers, etc.) and they formed "enTergy" teams to bring their idea to fruition.

Your detailed plan needs to include a detailed time line, as well. I like to manage my objectives (MBO), small management units connected with a deadlines. This enables you to measure or evaluate your success. It keep you moving toward your predetermined goals. Pharmaceutical companies imagine that it is possible to create drugs to cure diseases. They know those cures are out there, but they haven't found all of them yet. All of the ideas that come out of these imaginings will not be successful, but failure itself is not failure; it just eliminates some of the possibilities. We use this process: the "trial and error" method – to guide us toward success.

We cannot force things to be. We don't want to fool ourselves and disregard reality just to reach what we want to reach. If we find that the research and the experimentation do not point in the direction we want to go, we can't try to force it. Many people are so convinced that something should happen that they try to force it over again. Someone defined insanity as doing the same thing over and over, expecting different results. You must be able to discard ideas if they don't work out.

The Million Family March

I went to the Million Family March in Washington, D.C., in 2000. It was a lovely event. There were families of all types from all over who came to look for answers and issues about life as a family. On the Sunday of the same weekend, there was a Million Women March. There were females from 157 countries. They were women from all lifestyles and persuasions, from all parts of the world. They were discussing some of the terrible abuses that occur against women in underdeveloped and developed nations as well as injustices that happen in America. There was discussion of gender prejudice, class prejudice and racial prejudice. The theme was that you have to get rid of all the prejudice in the world, because all of us are God's children. Everybody has basic rights as a human being, and that's what America's all about. It was a wonderful conference, and the most important message I got out of it was if things are going to change, it's going to change by people who change them. When you are trying to resolve a problem, everybody has to leave the table with something. The rich have a mindset that is rational to them. Poor people have the rationale that is viable to them. What are the things that we have to get together on?

First, we can say that everybody has a right to certain things, and then you go from there. A guy who's paying a lot of taxes does not necessarily want the money to go to other people. On the flip side, the person who doesn't have much gets ticked off seeing people having $1,000 parties. Somebody has to be able to have the rich and the poor work together to come up with some type of workable plan. I think that can be done. I think it must be done. I don't know who that person is, but it seems that everybody at the Million Man March was receptive to the idea.

Cooperative competition

In a process I call "cooperative competition," everybody tries to do the best that he or she can. Naturally, there are always some losers (people who do not reach the top) but are helped by people who don't get to the top. It just keeps going and going, and that makes the pie bigger and bigger. All you need is to imagine and the ability to sit down and see what everybody needs, and then debate those issues rationally. Once you get the basic needs of everybody met, then you can use your remaining energy to pursue people's wants.

I think everybody should be rich. I think everybody should aspire to be rich. I found out a lot of rich people do a lot of things to help people in literature, architecture, philanthropy and many other areas, as well. I think rich people are great. I think people are great. I think that once you have a lot of money, you should use some of that money to help other people who have needs. Not necessarily individual donations, but put something into your legacy that will enable other people to move up. I don't have a lot of money, but I do give to a lot of charities, colleges and individuals. I try to do a lot of things to help others. I sit on a lot of boards. I enjoy doing that to because I think that's what the situation needs. To whom much is given, much is required.

Everything comes from imagination

There can be no process without imagination. There can be no creativity without imagination. Imagination fuels everything. Many things that we take for granted now we could have laughed off as crazy ideas a hundred years ago. The telephone? Television? Satellite communication? Someone's crazy idea today might sound crazy to us right now, but that believer thinks that it can be done. I don't think that there is anything that is impossible. I know we have physical laws and natural laws, but there are ways to get around them too. Anything's possible.

"Edu-car-letics"

You can be whatever you want to be. Many people come to college without any idea of what they want to do. They haven't even thought about it. The question has never gotten to them. One of the first assignments I give my new students is to write a 1-page autobiography and to include with their goals, where they are going to go, and what they are going to achieve in their ambitions. I'm creating an organization now that helps young people to focus on education, careers and athletics combined in one world. It's called "Edu-car-letics." All the youngsters in it know that they are in a basketball program that I assist with for the youth basketball leagues in the city of Raleigh, North Carolina. Currently we work with ages 10 to 13. We have little leagues, and through basketball, these youngsters learn critical life skills. Athletics are a very educational endeavor. First of all, they teach you how to work with a team (with other people). You all have several basic goals wrapped around one common goal, which is to win. They teach you how to be a team player. Second, they teach you the rules of the game. No matter what type of game you're in, there are certain rules and strategies that you have to obey. The third thing they teach you is that in order to win, you have to work as hard as you possibly can. You must focus on what you are doing. The fourth lesson is you must be in shape in order to win the game. Finally, the fifth, you've got to play as smart as you can. That means getting an education. You've got to be smart about the game. Those are the five lessons of Edu-car-letics. We're teaching them that they not only do they have to play athletics this way, but in education and career planning, they have to do the same thing. In order to play, in order to get to the pros, they have to go through school. Most of them do not have enough money to go to school on their own, so they have to get a scholarship. There are schools everywhere, and if a young person stays in our program and follows this plan, he or she stands a good chance of getting into college somewhere, through either athletic or academic ability. Some of them have great skills. I can tell that some of them are going to be great basketball players if they stay focused. Some of them know about the pro experience because their parents play or have played in college and in the NBA, and other kids are going to learn about it from them.

'Edu-car-letics" is going to prepare these kids for an education and for a career – a professional athletic career, if that's what they want, because although they come to play basketball, we also have computers and other learning resources available. We are including the whole family: parents and grandparents, everybody. Everybody plays: parents, grandparents, uncles, aunts, and interested neighbors. Then we eat hot dogs and hamburgers. We go on outings like camping trips and we have tournaments on the weekends with 25 or 30 teams invited from all over the area. We also invite people in to speak to the kids about certain things of importance in making them productive citizens. Those that want to play golf can use Meadowbrook county club, which is a country club owned by St. Augustine's University in Raleigh, North Carolina. Most people really don't know about Meadowbrook, which was built in 1958. We were unable to go to an all-Caucasian country club, so we build one for ourselves: tennis courts, swimming pool, everything. We didn't let our imaginations stop us from doing it. We just asked ourselves what we needed to do to get it done, and then we just went on and did it. You can do a lot of things if you just imagine you can do them, which is closely tied to your attitude. You can use imagination as a positive tool to get whatever you want, and imagination goes through all of the various aspects of our lives: imagination and attitude.

Creativity follows a passion

There is imagination, there's passion and then there's creativity. Passion is love for doing what it is you are doing, regardless of the monetary reward. Some people just enjoy doing what they are doing. I never felt like I worked a day in my life because I loved coaching and teaching. It was great that I happened to be paid for it, but had I not been paid well, I would have done it anyway. If you have a passion for something, you do it well. For it, you're going to get paid, because you're going to get better and better, and your product or service is going to be greater and greater demand.

You don't have to put any limits on your thinking, because you know it's always an infinite process. No matter if you come out undefeated, you know that the games still need to be taken to another level. You're never there. You're always in process of getting there. You've got to continually do better and better. That's only if you have the passion. Once the passion to go to higher levels leaves you, be comfortable where you are. To be comfortable without passion might lead you to incompetence.

Aspire to be successful (in some hierarchical pattern that includes spirituality, health, knowledge, wisdom, wealth and fame). Unfortunately, the vast majority of people aren't lucky enough to have found the things that they're passionate about, so they're still trying to figure out how to do that. They get caught up in whatever it takes to make a living, and sometimes that squeezes out the time for things they're passionate about. People think about making a living. People should be thinking about making a fortune. Then in the process, you'll make a living. You want to make a fortune. Make a fortune in what it is you do. If Tiger Woods can make a hundred million dollars hitting a golf ball, I know you can find something that you enjoy doing. Can you just imagine? It's almost insane when you think of it, that someone can make 100 million dollars hitting a golf ball. He's not making a living, although there are a lot of golfers that are playing who are just putting bread on the table.

A book for all families

I thought about this when I saw the Million Family March and all the things that the families were looking for. They seem to seek a definitive direction. They were all looking for guidance and providing answers to their problems. It helped put this project into a bigger perspective. It made me see the idea I designed to help all families everywhere: rich, poor, black, white, yellow, brown, wired, or unwired.

Some things to do

1. Can you imagine yourself outside-the-box?
2. Fantasize on what you would imagine yourself to be without limitations.
3. Write out what you have a passion to do and a plan for achieving it.
4. Go to the library. Talk with the librarians. Get on-line. Do research.
5. Find a good coach.
6. Do what you want to do.

CHAPTER 5

SOCIALIZING

Define it first

Webster's Dictionary defines sociality as "Pleasant companionship with ones friends and acquaintances; friendly relationships with others." My philosophy is that you should be sociable and social with everybody, unless you run into some things that would be detrimental to you, the other person, or organization. I think, first of all, you have to be sociable with yourself. It's very difficult to be social with someone else if you don't get along with yourself. Now that seems crazy, but what do I mean? I discovered early that if you are going to be happy, it's left up to you, not anyone else. Often, people think things like belonging to the right cliques, going to the best clubs, wearing the right clothes, and being invited to certain events are what makes you a person and what makes you happy. I don't think so. I think basically, deep down within, you have to be satisfied with yourself first, and you should be able to be social with yourself. Practice enjoying yourself with yourself as much as possible.

Socializing with yourself

I sometimes celebrate what I call "me days" and throw "me parties." My wife does the same thing. That means that today is my day. It's for me. It's going to be designed, by me for me. I'm going to have a good time with me. Sometimes you get caught up in the stresses of work, the family, and taking care of everybody else's business but yours, you feel uptight and you need to unwind and do some things for you. That's when you take this day and use it as you see fit. A "me day" is usually pretty unstructured. It's just whatever I want to do that day. I like to read and listen to good music. I like to play golf, and sometimes I just like to walk in the malls. Wherever my passion leads me for that day, that's what I'll do. I tell people, this is a "me day." I tell them, don't ask me to mow the lawn. Don't ask me to do a thing. I'm going to do whatever I want to do today, because I need to unwind.

Set the right tone with your children

Basically, we are social beings. We belong to and feel secure in groups. The natural order of things says that we grew up living in a communal-type atmosphere. Most of the social habits that we have come from first the family, then from the neighborhood and our friends, and so on. How we socialize our children in relationships with us goes a long way in determining how they're going to react to people. If we're uptight and "anti" and don't socialize well, or don't have what we call a pleasant personality (which we dealt with in the chapter on attitude), chances are our kids are going to be the same way. Sociality really begins in the home, the family, and then the neighborhoods. We don't need the Hatfields and the McCoys anymore.

More about "Edu-car-letics"

The "Edu-car-letics" program spoke about in the chapter on imagination mainly focuses on African-American males who like playing basketball. It is the city's game. I don't know if it's because we've lived primary in the inner cities, and by nature, living in inner city means that you have to be professional ball players. There are former players in the community whom the kids look up to and respect. What we try to do is get them together and form a league that plays in different areas. I give clinics to kids as young as 7 and as old as 18.

We stress how to behave like gentlemen, how to play with your team, and how to get along with your team mates. This is family. What we found out is once kids learn to play together, they learn how to behave in a group environment. They watch you very, very closely to see how you react. They watch to see if you have favorites: if a kid is playing because his daddy donates money to the YMCA, for example. We try to treat them all the same. We take them on outings to different places. We talk about being sociable, having a nice attitude. We try to create a model outside the home if there's not one in the home, because this learning must happen at an early age.

"Intergenerational Collaborative EnTergy"

As I said earlier in this book, there is another program, called "ICE" (that's "Intergenerational Collaborative EnTergy") in which we try to involve everyone that a kid interacts with. We hold social events in which we not only invite the kids, but also their parents and grandparents, and any other significant others. Because they like to play basketball, our motto is, "If you're not in the NBA, then as far as you can go." That tells people that we want excellence, and all of the attributes that go along with it. When the kids are playing having a good time, and when you eat and drink together, the parents have a tendency to meet and greet each other, too. Then we get a chance to tell them the things we are trying to do with the youngsters.

Basically there are 5 lessons to learn on the court:

- We want them to play together.
- We want them to play fair.
- We want them to play hard.
- We want them to play smart.
- We want them to play at increasingly skilled levels.

We also want them to get their education. We want them to have a spiritual awareness and know that there are inner resources within themselves that they can turn to when others don't understand their situations. Those are the values we try to instill. When we have tournaments on Saturdays or weekends with different groups and their parents, we have hot dogs and hamburgers, and sometimes we go out somewhere like pizza parlors. We don't place a lot of emphasis on who won or who lost. You had a good time. You played hard. You did the best you could. To us, that's what success is.

We try to put these leagues in faith communities, also. It works very well in Sunday schools and other youth development programs, and more churches are using athletics as a way of bring more youngsters into the church. In some of the churches we have computers, and we rotate the teams in and out to give the kids exposure to computers. We'll be teaching career skills for one hour while the others will be playing basketball and still others are on the computer. The next objective is to go to school and get teachers in on this. I think you have to integrate and cooperate with all the generations. Everybody has to work together as an "ICE"–team. The more people you involve, the better off it will be. Then you get to the colleges. You have the letterman clubs, sororities, and fraternities, and since the 60's, the social fellowship group. Social fellowship groups were developped for those kids whose parents didn't have the money it often takes to get into the sororities or fraternities, or they didn't have the GPA, but wanted to have a group to which they belonged. Everybody wants to feel like they belong.

The need to belong

In Maslow's Hierarchy of Needs, about third up on the hierarchy is the need to belong. That's why we have gangs, as long as those gangs are taught the things that they need to do to be productive. People usually assume a bad definition of what a gang is, but all it is, is a group of people who do similar things, who enjoy each other's company. As adults, we have to be able to see who the gang members are, try to get them to communicate with us, and then teach them positive things, rather than say, "Well, they're bad guys." They're bad guys because nobody has taken the time to sit down with them and ask them, "Hey, what is it that you guys want to do? Let's see what we can do constructively so that you can live a long productive life." We welcome gangs. We talk to people that might be in the gangs, and we try to do a positive turn around rather than being fearful of them. We include them in forums and talk and embrace them, also.

Socializing at home

I recently had a big birthday party where there were people from all over the world. It was an international party. My wife is a great entertainer and she put some snacks out on the deck; the food was in the dining room. We always have videotapes playing of various musical artists. We had Whitney Houston's latest video on in the sitting room upstairs. Downstairs we had the football game on for the guys who wanted to watch it. We had some little snacks in that room, and in the other den, my computer room, we had the beverages. The reason for spreading everything around the house was that it required everybody to move around and not stay in one place. If you don't do that, they'll get into a little pocket. When you put things in different places, they have to mingle to get them, and then they talk, introduce themselves, and everybody has a great time. This approach to social gatherings can be used in school, church, job, wherever. You need to know who your people are because you want to make sure you have a good cross section. At my party, everybody had a chance to mingle, and there were some very interesting conversations going on. It was also designed so that people couldn't just sit in one area. I always rent extra chairs, but I didn't put enough out to start with on purpose because I wanted people to stand up, mingle and walk around looking for an empty chair. After they had stood there for a little while, I would ask them, "Do you need a chair?" and I would get them one. I had 40 folding chairs outside in my van, but I took them out as I needed them so that when new people walked in, they initially didn't have a chair. They had to walk and hunt. We ultimately used all the 40 chairs, but I mixed the crowd up and encouraged conversation by parceling them out over the length of the party. That's an example of what I mean about being social.

Socializing across ethnic groups

I make a point of socializing with different races and ethnic groups regularly. Whether they are Caucasian, Latin, Asian, or Hispanic, I like going to their events and just walk around to meet friends and smile. Sometime they get a little amazed and confused as to why I'm there, but that doesn't matter to me. I meet new people, have a lot of fun, and life doesn't become boring. I tell my wife "We're going to out for Mexican tonight," or "We're going out country and western style tonight." The people usually will become friendly if you're friendly. I tell them, "This is the first time I've ever been here and can you teach me how to do this?" or I watch the room to see who's amiable and who smiles and who waves and who seem approachable. If somebody has an attitude, I definitely do not ask that person for any kind of assistance. I've found that most of the time they're curious and want to know who you are and why you came. By doing this, it helps me understand how other people feel, how they do things, and then I can invite them to my affairs, too. I always carry my personal business cards in my pocket. I have several different business cards. I give them one and say, "Give me a ring if I can help you."

Sociability on the job

Being sociable on the job means getting along with your co-workers. Since most businesses are focused on bottom line and quarterly results, I think there should be some type of social gathering for employees at the end of the quarter to let them know that what they are doing is appreciated and how it can be improved upon. The company may or may not have reached its targets. If they did reach them, well good; they can have a great party. If they fell short, then they can discuss how to do better the next quarter. Recognizing that morale might be down a little bit, management could explain the reasons they didn't get to the goal. They should reinforce the fact that they're a team and they're going to have this social or family gathering regardless of the bottom line. I think a corporation that plays together prosper together, and I think the CEO should be there, along with his or her managers, and they should have a family good time. At the same time management can get all the teams together, when everybody is feeling good, and let them know where you are, what you are doing, and what your prospects are for the next quarter. The managers should recognize the contributions of their staff and ask them to stand up and be recognized. They should also share what the projections are for the next quarter and engage the team in discussing ways to ensure that they make their targets. This kind of ritual is important for team spirit because although people work together, they often don't socialize together. Once they have a chance to socialize together, they find out that they're basically all the same.

What kind of day do you want it to be?

It's a beautiful day if you decide it is. I read the newspapers on the weekends because they list what's going on in the area, and we just arbitrarily pick something we want to do, and just go. It's just beautiful. What I'm trying to say in a nutshell is that it's left up to you just how sociable you're going to be and how you're going to relate to others. You go to them. Don't look for them to come to you. You always have to take the initiative to do anything if you want to enjoy life. Don't ever look to anything else to make things happen for you. You have to make them happen. God doesn't make bad days. I counsel people against trying to bring bad days to me.

Some things to do

1. How would you describe yourself socially – shy or outgoing?
2. How do you fit in social gatherings?
3. What would you like to improve socially?
4. How do you feel in racially diverse settings?
5. Write out how you can improve?
6. Go to the library. Talk to the librarians. Get online. Do research.
7. Find a good coach.
8. Do what you want to do.

HARVEY D. HEARTLEY, SR.

CHAPTER 6

EDUCATION

What is it?

Webster's Dictionary defines education as "The action or process of educating or being educated; a field of study dealing with the methods of teaching and learning; to provide someone with schooling; to develop mentally and morally; to provide information; to instruct, teach." One of the school superintendents with whom I worked told me that his definition of education was, "Teachers teaching and students learning." I personally prefer a little broader definition: I do what is needed when it needs to be done, whether you want to or not. It can be in either a formal or an informal setting. It's finding out the specific skills that are needed to perform a certain task, developing them, and changing your behavior. I don't think you can be truly educated if your behavior doesn't change.

When I was teaching health classes, we would do self- inventory. Some of the students smoked. After we had completed the textbook chapter on smoking, I would expect that if the students understood the ramifications of smoking, they would know that smoking is not good for them. If they hadn't quit smoking by the time the semester ended, I didn't know whether they had been educated, or not. I put much more emphasis on "How is your behavior?" than on "What do you know?"

Infinite processing

My philosophy of living is, "Every day, in every way, I am getting better and better and better." We can never stop learning (educating ourselves). Living is a life-long learning process; a journey, not a destination. Enjoy the journey.

Bloom's taxonomy of learning

Bloom classified learning into six parameters. The first memory: you have to be able to memorize information in order to go on to the next step, which is comprehension. After you have memorized it, can you comprehend what it means? The next level in Bloom's taxonomy is: can you use the information? Then comes analysis: can you take the information apart to see how it is put together? Next comes synthesis, which I believe is the most important step, because now you're creating. You've taken something that you learned and you've used it. You're taking it apart and now you're going to take it to another level: you're going to create something new or better out of it. For example, first there was the typewriter, then came the telegraph, the computer, the Internet, and everything has continued to improve over time. Now we have computers, and second and third generation memories about them, etc. This is what Bloom was talking about. The last step in Bloom's taxonomy is evaluating. Can you judge whether it was good or bad, or whether it was neutral in its effect on the larger community, not necessarily just you. I've added a seventh step, which I say is refining, and that means you're getting better and better and better in creating a better you and a better society. You are increasingly able to make the people around you better.

Life-long learning

It's a beautiful day when you talk to these youngsters, or anyone, about life-long yearning. It never stops. There's always something you're interested in. Not the same thing all the time; eventually you'd get bored with that. When you look at the different parameters of something, it makes life exciting and enjoyable cause when you go to bed at night and you're analyzing your day.

You say, "Tomorrow I think I'll learn about this or I'll do that." It's really an exciting way to live life because there's always something new out there, and you're getting a new education at the same time. Once again, the setting doesn't have to be a formal one. You can learn wherever you are. All the world is a classroom.

Making time for education

Regardless of whether it's formal or informal, there are 168 hours in each week for everybody, all over the world. What you do to educate yourself in those 168 hours, whether it's on a job, in a sport, or in the classroom, you have to determine how you are going to use your time to get educated. (See daily activity schedule at the beginning of this book). Given the fact that we all have to sleep, I normally think of the day as being from 6:00 a.m. to 11:00 p.m. That's the general time frame we have to work with. Normally in America, the workday starts between 7 to 9 in the morning and you generally work 8 hours a day. Of course, self-employed people may not have this kind of predictable and controllable schedule. If you are going to fit education into that limited time frame, you've going to have to have a certain time that you have to get up, do your grooming and get to the job or wherever you need to go. During the hours that are available to you for learning, you have to decide what you really want to do. Use your discretionary time wisely and to your development.

Your daily activity schedule

At the beginning of every class of every semester I taught, I had the students write their autobiographies. This was a way to find out who they were and to tell them who I was. I wanted to hear from them about their plans. They were there to get an education, and I knew from experience that most people did not manage their time effectively. In order to educate them about time management, I gave them each to fill out a form every week for the first 30 days of class: their daily activity schedule. At the end of each week, I would take them up and review them. They would fill in their class schedules and when they were going to study for each class.

It's usually a good idea to study right after class because the material is on your mind. I would tell them I was programming them to make A's in all their classes. I would say, "Right now, you have an A in my class. If you follow your daily activity schedule, do what you are supposed to do, and turn in your assignments, then you got a round map on how to be an A student." I explained why they were required to review their schedules for the first week every month, because it forced them to look back and see what they hadn't got done. "You'll get behind," I'd say. "Catch-up belongs to hotdogs and hamburgers. It's a hard game to play." I know, I'm a coach. There's very little structure in college, especially when you are dealing with first-generation college students whose parents didn't go.

This approach to time management can be geared to a work schedule, as well. It doesn't matter where you are. Among other things, their schedules need to include a hour every day to keep fit. Everything was left up to the students. I believe in making people responsible for their own choices and not necessarily trying to tell them what to do. In order to teach the student to manage their study time effectively, I developed a concept called "study buddies." Each student had to pick someone in the class with whom to study, and they had to go over their activity schedules together and give each other feedback. Some of them were married with jobs, some of them participating in athletics, and I could see that they were headed for breakdowns if their activities took up so many hours that they couldn't get enough rest. This personal discipline of the daily activity schedule is important because I think education and most things are best done when there is a process – process education.

Rules for learning

When every semester began, I introduced my students to several tools for learning, the first of which was " the 3 P's." Every day, I told students they need to be:

- Present
- Punctual, and
- Prepared

I drummed these words into them so often that after a few weeks, all I had to do was hold up three fingers and they would know what I meant. Sometimes there were "5 P's," meaning:

- Prior preparation prevents poor performance.

There are 3 very important rules I tried to teach to all my students:

- **Rule 1:** "Keep your mouth closed, observe and learn."

- **Rule 2:** "Keep your nose out of other folks business unless they beg you or pay you."

- **Rule 3:** "Research, plan, and produce."

I always told my students that if they could follow and control the first, that meant a BS degree; if they could do both 1 and 2, that meant a Master's degree, and if they could follow all 3 rules, that would mean a Ph.D. Sometimes a student would come up to me and say, "Coach, I still have to pass rule 1. I can't keep my mouth closed. I'm not even thinking about rule 2!"

Life-long learning starts at an early age

My philosophy is that we should improve daily, and that it is a never ending process. "Every day, in every way, I am getting better and better and better" such that you develop a love for education. I think that people have to develop a love for it if they're going to do things that are exciting and that they consider as self-improving. That concept has to be fostered in the schools. There are all kinds of schools of thought on education, but I think first of all there has to be desire, and that has to come from the individual. They have to be motivated: intrinsically or extrinsically.

Educating children and teaching them the love of learning is critical. Parenting is a key way in which children learn, as is the school system. I'm going to list the major goals of the American school system, adding my own interpretation of each. The first is to achieve "mastery of basic skills, of the fundamental processes" (I call that "reading, writing and arithmetic"). Next is career or vocational education. In other words, an individual person's satisfaction with life will be significantly related to the persons job satisfaction (That's what I call a "decent job"). "Intellectual development" is the next goal. Life is complex, and I say, "you need to know what time it is." "Enculturation" refers to the individual's relationship with other people, the entire society, our values, etc., his or her sense of belonging (My interpretation is that "you need to be able to get along with other people"). "Autonomy" means that you need to be competent in dealing with certain individuals responsibilities and have the ability to learn on your own (I consider that "self- reliance"). "Citizenship" means that we need people who can be good citizens and people who can be good citizens and participate in the political process (I call that "a good, productive participating citizen"). "Creativity and aesthetic perception" means "appreciation for fine arts." "Self-concept" means that you need to be able to have your own personal goals and aspirations and to have a healthy sense of yourself (which I call "self-esteem"). "Emotional and physical well-being," I call a "healthy individual." "Moral and ethical character" means we need to be able to not necessarily to determine right from wrong, because those definitions change as time goes on, but to those things that society had found to be best everybody at this point in time (To me that means "decent moral values"). The next goal is "self-realization," and I like to use the phrase the U.S. Army coined, "Be all you can be." I want to add a last goal, which is "spiritual awareness." The school system has trouble including this one because of legal rulings, but I believe this is one of the most important aspects what we need from education.

Intergenerational Collaborative "EnTergy" (ICE')

Education in the schools will be enhanced or most

effective when we educate the parents along with the students. I have a process called "intergenerational collaborative enTergy," which addresses that need. When I say "intergenerational," I'm thinking there should be a link of various people from conception through death. I like to think back to what I called the natural order of things. That means that before we could conceptualize it, it existed. It patterned a natural order. I can't say that God ordained it, but if we didn't know things, there would be some type of order that would just take place instinctively, in a Darwin-type way. If you go back to the first man and woman (I don't know whether they were Adam or Eve or not, but there had to be a first male and female at some point in time), they existed as community. They got older and they had children. Then you had a group of people who were just developing, and they were within one content. For survival, some had to work, some had to have the children, and somebody was going to die. The people who started living first knew a lot about what was going on than others, so talking and using a language to communicate must have been only at the most rudimentary level. Language had to be developed later. They figured out what needed to be done, and they did it such that everybody in the clan or tribe could survive. The elders, for the most part, did the education of the young, because they had the time and wisdom. I believe we still need that type of relationship. It doesn't necessarily have to be family, but there needs to be an attachment (an interconnecting relationship) between people from the time a child is born to the time he/she dies.

Somewhere in society – in family, in the school system, or the church, or somewhere else – we need to let everyone know that people always need help and assistance and there is a network for you. Your children never actually grow up completely. They're your children forever. I don't think people have this mindset when they get married or start a family, but I firmly believe the philosophy that, "They're my children, and as long as I'm living it is my responsibility to continue to teach them, to help them if they want to learn." I have always tried to be open and available to let my children know that if they have a problem, they can always bring it to Daddy. That doesn't mean I'm going to automatically solve it for them, but I'm always there to talk and to give guidance and support. Somehow or another, we have to develop this philosophy in the community, and I believe it can be done best through the faith organizations. I am personally very active in a number of faith groups and other community organizations. We try to get the message in the church and in the schools that everybody needs some help, and we're here to help and serve one another. Unless we can do something to educate and assist parents, they will not be able to educate their children, in turn. I think retired people are the most valuable reservoir of knowledge we have. We need to have more and better ways to take advantage of all better ways to take advantage of all they have to offer our young people. We find that if we develop a relationship between the youngsters and the senior citizens (the grandparents) then we get the parents involved, too. Everybody learns.

<u>A gift from my parents</u>

I always had varied interests. I thank God that my mother and father were both teachers. There were always books in our home; there was always learning there. There was very little radio and no television when I was a child. I played ball and studied. That was all I did. I knew my daily activity schedule, even though I didn't know that's what it was). I knew when I was going to get up in the morning, when I was going to school, when I was going to come home and do my chores, and after that, when I was going to do my homework. Then I knew I was going to go out and play. Then I was going to come inside and eat dinner, and then I was going to do some studying. Then at 9 the lights were going out and I was going to be going to sleep. That's just the way it was. I have a lot of respect for young people today because there are so many things out there now that were not here when I was growing up. There were no drugs that we knew of; there was alcohol, but nobody made it available to kids; there were gangs, but good gangs. It was just a great time.

Some things to do

1. Go to the local library; get a library card if you don't have one.
2. Make sure all family members do the same.
3. Plan a family trip to your local library.
4. Have the library take you on a library tour explaining all the services available to you.
5. Log on your computer and browse the internet.
6. Schedule a family library party.
7. Find a good coach.
8. Do what you want to do.

Chapter 7

MENTALITY

What does it mean?

Webster's Dictionary defines it as "Relating to the mind's capacity; how much it can absorb." In my own definition, I think mentally is one's ability to deal with abstract and practical matters such that are in his or her best interest. It sometimes can be referred to as IQ, meaning a tangible way to test one's ability to deal with finite and abstract things. There are different lines of thoughts regarding whether IQ can be improved. Some researchers say that what you're born with, what your parents bring to the table genetically, is basically what you're going to have. I've found that people have different intelligence quotients on different things. Some people look at that as aptitude and achievement. Those are rather nebulous works, because when you start dealing with one's mental capacity, there are a lot of things that play in one's ability to comprehend (such as diet, environment, school environment, and so forth). The main thing I want people to know is that they do have a mental component that they should try to develop as much as they possibly can. Without that there are limits, because I think that the only limits that exist as anything are in one's mind. As long as you can let your mind flow, anything is possible. I'm not saying that if you have an IQ of 80, you're going to be a rocket scientist. I am saying that you should never limit yourself or your children or anybody based on what the IQ test (or SATs) states. It all depends on the individual capacity. The message that I want to get across is that there are no limits. Developing your mentality is an infinite process.

In developing the mental aspect, you also have to consider the emotional aspect. *Webster's Dictionary* defines emotional as: "intense feelings of love, pain, fear, jealousy." As long as you're aware those feelings exist, you'll be all right. I think that the only two real emotions are love and fear; all the rest are ramifications of either incomplete or distorted love or fear. I might even want to go a little further and say the only true emotion is love. If love is there, all those other things will cease to exist. I don't think they really exist in nature. If you look at an animal, they don't really have any fear.

Those are learned emotions. Many mental illnesses come from emotions that we have engendered somewhere along the way, and these fears often affect our mental picture of how things need to be. I think a lot of the time we put too much emphasis on one's ability to handle things from a mental standpoint, and we frighten people.

Setting the right tone with children

The way that parents socialize their children can set them up to fail. This happens, for example, if the adult in the child's life is always telling them, "Don't do this. You can't do that!" and they are bombarded with negatives. Another example is if they're always talked down to: "Shut up. Sit down. Be quiet." I think in the school system, use of drugs for hyperactivity and the things that they do to inhibit kids' movement creates a problem not only for their mentality, but also for their physicality. I think that the mentality of the kids now is pretty sharp. It's just that I don't think we know how to tap into that mentality. If the situations in the mental setting are depressing, you set people up for anxieties and neuroses, and eventually psychoses and nervous breakdowns. We're living in a highly, highly complex world now, and you've got to bring something to the table. We can start by letting people know that they do have capacities, and regardless of what it is supposed to be on the paper, they can be pretty much what they want to be. If the individual is interested and the people that are dealing with them are interested, then I think they may have what they need to make a reasonable living in society. You can be what you "work" to be.

Mentality and morality

Within the context of mentality we find morality, too. Morality comes from one's ability to distinguish between right and wrong. According to *Webster's Dictionary*, morality is "The principles to right and wrong," or "Conforming to a standard of supposedly rightly conceived behaviors." You have to be really careful when you start dealing with moral issues, because what is cultural today might be unacceptable tomorrow, and vice versa. My philosophy is that those things that are in the best interests of the larger universe are usually what's moral and what is not. Those things that are self-serving to an individual or group might not be moral in the larger framework, so you might be very careful with your moralities. Before you try to develop hard definitions of what's right and what's wrong, you have to look at it in a very, very empathetic light.

It's very difficult to deal with emotional, moral issues without using the mentality that you bring to the table, such as logical thought, or trying to think outside the box. Using this approach is going to make your life either more pleasurable or it's going to create some psychic problems for you. Emotions alone can be problematic if you don't balance them with some logical and intellectual thinking. If you feel that your emotional state is out of balance, step back, think more logically, honestly and objectively, and give yourself some time; you can get a good balance between the two, the mental and emotional.

Empathy and sympathy comes into the picture, too. It's possible to go too far on the logical, thinking side, and lose the common touch.

Mentality in business

The business side of mentality depends on your philosophy as a person. A friend of mine is a high-level executive at a company he's been at for 30 years. When he first started out, he was a primary bottom-line man. Then they restricted, downsized, and "bottom-lined" so much that it began to hurt and he began to leave them. They went to competitors, and their stock is way down now. He had a lot of stock options, and, of course, they dropped in value. He found out that some of the people had been loyal and receptive to the company didn't feel that way anymore. When they had a hurricane or flood and he wanted to get this group together, some of them didn't want to work, making overtime. He said he remembered the time when the relationship between management and the workers were so good that they would have gotten together, just for him. After so much disruption and change, they felt differently. He said he was beginning to see and understand what I had been talking about for years (BUPL).

Balancing logic and emotions

After thinking about the issues for a number of years, although it doesn't really lean itself to a formula, I think that a 50/50 approach is best: try to weigh in evenly with logic and emotions. If you err, err on the side of emotions, because people usually don't have the same logical thought. That fluctuates. When it gets to feelings, what hurts you is usually going to hurt me, too. I try to empathize or put myself in the situations of others regularly. Sometimes I want to embrace Mexican culture, so I'll do that for that day. I'll eat at a Mexican café. I'll go out to one of the entertainment places wearing Mexican attire. I have a great time. Sometimes I go country and western, too. I can tap and clog and do all of that. I think if you have a global mentality, you'll be able to handle things pretty well. I find that you can't change people's mentality most of the time, but stay aware of local mentality. If you throw some open-ended questions out, without making any judgments, and let them think about them, most people will rise to the occasion. People, for the most part, are good. I assume everybody is good. I think there are good people who have bad ideas, or somewhere along the lines they've gotten things all mixed up. I hope this book will let them look at themselves in a new light, because really what we're doing is dissecting self and seeing how we react to these things.

There is a lot of linkage between the relationship area that I talked about earlier and this area, in that if something is awry about a relationship, it can feel like an emotional thing. You have to step back and do some logical thinking. That helps you have a better perspective on relationships. If you don't do that, you will create stress.

Mentality and stress

Stress is defined by *Webster's Dictionary* as "Any force that induces bodily or mental tension," or what I call change in balance. If I'm at rest and I get up and go out the door, that creates stress. Not enough stress to create the problem, but it causes the heart rate to go up, and so forth and so on. It's always important that you understand the physical implications of what's going on. How is it affecting you? For example, if I'm in great shape, I can handle a lot more stress, a lot more emotional tension, than I can if I'm not. I'm not saying physical fitness is more important than mental fitness, but the fact is if you're dead, you can't handle any of them.

Most of the time stress is transitory, but if it lasts a period of time, it brings on sickness. I don't think we'll ever be able to eliminate drugs, because when people get very stressed, they feel they need to do something to help them get back down to a state of tranquility. Some people use exercise; some people do sports; some read; but drugs seem to do it immediately, if not sooner. We spend 60 billion dollars in America on illegal drugs, and I don't know how much on legal drugs. Statistics show that Americans, for the most part, spend most of their drug money on prescription drugs. Drugs let people feel good and pretend to be whoever they want to be. That's a very powerful argument. They become addicted to tranquilizers and antidepressants.. I'm not talking about junkies. Those are the ones you see on the news and you read about, but that is only the tip of the iceberg. It's the people that are making big money on stressful jobs who are able to handle their habits that you don't see. Most of the people who get picked up are the ones who are visible; the ones on the street. In some of the courses I taught, we talked about consumer health, and the fact that when you watch television, there's a pill for everything that exist. If you're scratching your nose or have a little allergy, you can get a little nose spray. Eyestrain? Put some eye wash in. If you have a little cramp, you can rub on a little cream. There is instant relief for whatever ails you; it's a pill generation.

The mentality to stand on your own

Our mental state is usually affected by our physical and emotional state, and our emotional state is somewhat influenced by our mental state. When I was teaching, the high school curriculum prepared a youngster at the end of freshman year to be able to go out and fend for himself, knowing the things that he need to know to be a self-sustaining person. Your emotions are always going to come into play. Whatever you're able to resolve mentally will be best for you versus what you want emotionally is something that's going to bother you as long as you live. It's not necessarily going to be a problem for a college student or somebody first starting out. It's something that is pervasive in all areas, because when you grow up, you should know better, but we know that that's not necessarily the case. Hopefully most people will learn early that you cannot live too far beyond your immediate income. Emotionally you might want to stretch that. Self-discipline and the ability to be able to look at something and see which is logical and which is emotional, those problems are going to always exist. I don't care how young you are or how old you get. You have to look at how it is going to affect you down the road. What's going to happen, and also think about all the bad things that can happen. Look at what the worst thing is that can happen. Although you really can't even imagine what the worst is, you have a pretty good idea. If that happens and you can deal with it, then you might go ahead. If you cannot resolve the worst case scenario, it's best for you not to do it. Some people say you shouldn't bite off more than you can chew. I say bite off more than you can chew and chew it. If you really want to do it, find a way to chew it.

Mental illness

"Normal" only means what is average, what the average person does. There are some people – many people – who will develop some type of illness that prevents them from acting and living "normally." Sometimes it is due to disease; sometimes it is due to stress; sometimes a mental illness will progress from anxiety to high anxiety, to inability to cope, to neurosis, to psychosis, to eventually suicide. If you have someone in the family or on the job who is under undue stress, usually the first, best person to talk with is your husband or wife, or mother, father, or somebody that you feel close to. Often people just need somebody to talk to, somebody they can sit down with and not worry about being judged or having their private conversations shared with others. Just talk to them and let them know what you think the situation is. You may be right, or might not be, but at least you can tell them what you feel. Usually things start first with feelings, and then from feelings you go to logic. Ministers are available, counseling areas are available, and so are clinics. There are a lot of places you can go for mental health problems. Generally speaking, you want to go to the minister first, then the literature, then you go to the web, and then you go to the experts. Then you go to the local people that have proven that they have had good experience with handling the particular type situation. That doesn't mean that you can just go to any minister, because some might exacerbate the problems. If your friends can not help you, perhaps they can refer you to someone who can. I don't know much about psychiatry and psychotherapy. They're OK if you got the money, but most of the time people don't have money to seek those options. There are health agencies within all counties where you can go and get help if you need it.

Screening for mental difficulties

There are mental tests available, and in college in the freshmen wellness classes, there is a section that deals with mental health. I would suggest that all families purchase a health book from the neighborhood book store. There is a self-assessment test that enables students to know if they have certain problems or tendencies and what to do to address them. You must be mentally sound in order to deal with the other aspects of your life, so beware of potential problems that are essential to every person, regardless of age or situation.

Some things to do

1. Go to the library and research the internet for materials to enhance your mental capacity.
2. Share with your family.
3. Talk to the family members about the importance of developing their mental capacity infinitely.

4. Find a good coach.
5. Do what you want to do.

Chapter 8

PHYSICAL FITNESS

What is it?

The dictionary defines the physical as "Development and care of the body ranging from simple calisthenics to training in health, fitness and hygiene." I believe that the physical is the incarnation of the spiritual. Because I'm a physical being, I'm also a spiritual being. I think spirituality is in the place called heaven, and there's a Harvey Heartley already up there, and that what he is contemplating from the mind and the spirit is being acted out down here. I don't necessary know that that's where I'm going when my body dies. The body is simply a vehicle to enable you to carry out your thoughts and your words in another realm. Be that as it may, we are physical. We are born into the world, and there are certain things we need to function and do whatever it is we want to do. Specifically, I'm talking about rest, food, lifestyle and, to make sure that the physical level is being maintained at the optimum level, exercise. We know from Maslow's Hierarchy of Needs that we've got to have air, water, food, and sex. Those needs are programmed on our hard drives.

We also need to rest, something I don't think Americans get enough of. In college, most of the students come to class sleepy, and without eating breakfast. They've broken 2 of the cardinal rules of maintaining the physical self. They haven't gotten proper nutrition and they haven't gotten proper rest. In addition to needing good nutrition and enough rest, the body is a machine and it works better when it's exercised. With computers, cars, elevators, and video games pervasive, we often do not get the exercise we need to keep our bodies going like they should. The fourth component that is critical to maintaining ourselves physically is avoiding excesses in the area of alcohol, sex and drugs. This is not a textbook on these subjects, but I want to let you know that they do exist and you have to know what your philosophy is on your physical health, per se. What do you know about it? What is your philosophy? What is your philosophy on rest? What is your philosophy on nutrition? What is your philosophy on exercise? Once you get to those things, you can go to the literature to find out what's what. Even if you don't think you have a philosophy, you do; it's just not defined and you are not aware of it.

I think that people should visit their libraries about once a week. I have textbooks that I've taught from for years, but numerous books are available in the library. People should do quick studies if they don't have time to read several books on a particular subject. Go to a book store, the college bookstore, to a library, or go on line to look up fitness and whatever subject in the category you want to learn about. You can get a quick capsulated update.

My own philosophy on physical fitness

If you're feeling good physically and you are able to work what I call a 'normal day" (8AM-6PM) with enough energy left at the end of the day to socialize or engage in some leisure time activities or recreation for two or three hours (which you need to sort of regenerate yourself) you'll be all right. Ask yourself how you feel. Are you able to carry on a normal workday, whatever your work is, with enough energy at the end of the day for recreation or activities with the family? If you can say yes to that question, you should be in pretty good physical shape. There is a new trend in corporations to work for 4, 10-hour days, and other flexible hours formats. The research is not clear on how that's going to affect people over a period of time. There will be an increase in stress, people might find that they get lazy on their days off, or they may be able to get enough rest working 10-hour days. It will take several years of research to really tell what the impact of this tend really is.

There's a lot of money spent on physical fitness. Everywhere you look there's a spa or a fitness center. A lot of churches have fitness centers that do walkathons and other events. There's a wealth of information out there on this subject. Then to maintain that good health, get your medical check-up regularly.

Give your body a healthy routine

Many people feel tired all the time. If you do, how do you go about resolving it? Most of the time, the problem is not enough rest. You should have a special time that you go to bed at night and a special time that you wake up, because your body is a creature of habit. Some people say, "I don't need but 6 hours of sleep; I don't need but 7. Some people need 8 or 9." 8 hours of sleep is the general rule of thumb, and I'm talking about deep sleep. If you get 8 good hours of sleep, where 6 of those are what we call REM sleep (Rapid Eye Movement), that's usually a good night's sleep. We've got to cut the TV off and eliminate all distractions in order to get good rest. If you short-change yourself and don't get enough rest, stress is going to come up. All types of things will happen to you and you may not be aware of why they are happening. The structure of the brain and the nervous system is such that all of those things that were primitive, we still have. They are still in the back of our brains. We're the only beings that develop a big forebrain from the spine. Everything that's autonomic, like our breathing and moving our legs, is handled by the ganglia in the back of our brains and all the front brain is mainly for the creative type things. We didn't really develop a complex brain until we decided we wanted to become human, because everything else was programmed. We did it by instinct. Those prehistoric traits are still there. As evolution has added on to it and added on to it, the brain has developed, and developed. We have taken on what we call humanistic characteristics. Under certain pressures, we can revert right back to those things that the animals used to do.

Everyone needs to know that there is a physical area of their life that needs to be finely tuned and you need to be intelligent about all of this. You can take it as far as you want to take it in either direction: you can look like a body builder or you might look teeny weeny. You can be healthy in either instance, but there are certain basic things that everybody needs to do.

Set an example for your children

Most of our philosophies come from our parents. We are bought up in a household and we, as children, usually by example, do what our parents do. We don't necessary do what they say to do. We hear what they say, but children are always watching the grownups. If they are living a good physical life, your children will do that, too. If you have a bed time for them, a time for them to get up, structure around when they eat, if they exercise, and if they get their physicals, then you will be teaching them how to live a physically sound life. If they see you staying away from inordinate amounts of alcohol, cigarettes or drugs, chances are they're going to do that, too. There's an old saying: actions speak louder than words. Problems with alcohol, tobacco and drugs can happen at an early age – especially alcohol and tobacco. We see them advertised; we see people use them (role models) where it's made to look chic, but it's against your best interest to use those things. The daily activity schedule that we have has a little section in it that asks you what your views are on this subject, and how you handle things. It's called a health assessment. In any good health book on the web, you can make an assessment of your health, and it will ask you if you use these things, if you don't use them, or if you use them in moderation. That is a big part of your physical health, because you can slide into abuse very, very easily. I'm not even going to get into that here, but you need to know that there are programs out there and you need to know how to get into them. Prevention is the best thing. When it comes to any detrimental acts, the best thing is to prevent it from happening.

When you don't take care of yourself, it shows

I taught health for 40 years. When you teach, you observe youngsters and you find out a lot about their lifestyles. You observe their eyes. You observe if they're sloughing, if they're asleep, if they have any particular nervous tics, if they're in class on time, if they seem to be hungry, and what they talk about. College students usually do not get enough rest, and usually they do not get the proper food. Although there is a dining hall available, if students have 8 classes and they get up later than they should, they don't eat breakfast, and it starts to show. They start "nabbing" (what I call eating nabs). Often, they're away from home for the first time, and before they know it, it's midterms and they have tried to get acclimated. They'll come tell me, "Coach I've got a problem." Some of them will have drug problems. Some of them will have sexual problems. Because some of them were not bought up in an environment of informed, knowledgeable parents, they don't really know what's going on. When they get on the college campus with people from everywhere, all over the country, they are apt to take the path of least resistance. They're nice students, and then all of a sudden, they're in trouble.

In my classes, students had to tell me their weekly plans. They had to fill out what I called a daily activity schedule, and then they had to look at the 13 cardinal principles of education so when they left school, they made sure that at least they knew what they were. Then I gave them a health and fitness guide. It showed them how to structure their lives based on 10 hour days: what time you get up, etc. They had to fill those out for me every day for a month, and then after that, they did it each month. The purpose was to give them a monthly checklist of what they were doing in their classes, their work, their sleep, and other elements of their lives. They had to get up in front of the class and talk to people about those things. For some of them, it was the first time they had that kind of structure. Not only the younger students, but the adult students, too.

When you are teaching and coaching and you're the Athletic Director as well as a family man, you have to have some structure, because if you don't, you've got a big blob of chaos. People don't function well in chaos. If you know what you got to do, when you got to do it, chances are, you'll do it. If you don't have structure, it can get away from you in a moment's time. I carry a little card with me every day that tells me what I'm supposed to do that day. The a.m. is on one side and the p.m. is on the other side. If I get distracted or off schedule, I can always go back to that card and get my day back in order. At the end of the day, I take a look at it to see how my day went and see how I wanted it to go. Then the next day when I get up, I know what didn't get done. I know whether I'm going to feel good or whether I ran my mouth and didn't do much.

I don't let myself get away with much. My high

school coach always told me, "You might fool some people. I don't recommend that you fool anybody," he said, "But don't ever fool yourself." You have to keep examining your life because a lot of times, we fool ourselves and we don't know we're doing it. It's easy to do. That whole denial thing is very powerful.

Handling health problems

There are four ways that we handle any health problem: prevention, education, treatment and rehabilitation. We call this "PETR." First, we try to prevent it. We try to use the vaccination, or whatever. Then we educate people on it so that they are aware of what's out there. Then, if those two don't take care of it, then we have to treat it. Finally, there's rehabilitation.

Your job can affect your physical self

There are some instances when people will put you in a position that you either don't have the skills or the desires to do. Once you get there, you'll find that this is really not where you should be. You usually end up in that situation because there's more money or more prestige in the new position. Finding yourself in the wrong job can cause heart attacks and stress. It's not necessarily the job that causes physical problems, it's the fact that you are not equipped to deal with the job, either in a skilled form or passion for work. Some people strive in high stress jobs, and some don't. my wife use to say, "You go all the time! It's basketball, basketball.... You're going all the time! Slow down, relax, live like normal people." It was a problem for her, but not for me. I enjoyed that. My son said I just liked the action. I do.

Some things to do

1. Look at the do-it yourself fitness guide in the quick-look section.
2. Visit the local library and the World Wide Web articles, books, tapes, and videos on fitness programs.
3. Check your daily activities schedule and find time for workouts.
4. Design your own fitness program.
5. Find a good coach.
6. Do what you want to do.

Chapter 9

FINANCES

Define it first

According to *Webster's Dictionary*, finance is "The management of money affairs, based on the resources that are available." I think that the ability to have resources available as a result of managing your affairs comes in a timely fashion, but it is also wise always to have more than you need. That's financial health: to have it whether you need it or not. That's my philosophy.

Linkage between finance and lifestyle

How you manage the money or resources that are available to you as a person is going to determine whether you have a nice, pleasant life, or whether you are going to be running from the collectors. My philosophy on finance is that you should choose work doing something that you like, and find someone willing to pay you enough money to live the lifestyle you think you should have.

Usually, the problem in the financial arena is not that we don't have enough money. It's that the things that we want far outstrip our ability to buy them. That is mainly because of television and other ways that we are exposed to how other people live who make a lot more money than we do ("the Joneses"). We want those lifestyles, and there's nothing wrong with aspiring to any type of lifestyles. There are various lifestyles that you can have based on the money that you have. It's like in athletics: you can be participatory, you can be competitive, or you can be the champion. All of them come with different payrolls.

Personal financial planning

As soon as you become employed, or you have resources coming in (you might have already have some that is left to you, for example) you should have a financial plan. You should know where your money is going to be coming from, weekly, monthly, or however you're being paid. Once that money is coming in, you should track it for about 6 months to see how much is coming in and how much is going out. You have to have a financial plan – most people call it a budget. I don't like to use the word "budget" because it frightens people. They think of a lot of numbers, sophisticated formulas and calculations. I recommend that you use a very simplistic way of tracking your finances. I always start at the beginning of the month, because the calendar is always organized. You always know when September or October is always coming. If you can start at the beginning of the month, it would give you a pretty good idea of what funds comes in during the month.

It's very simple to get a sheet of paper and put down the beginning of the month: October 1. You have little columns, you get a little inexpensive book, and you have what you owe, what you paid, what your balances are, and the check number or money order that you paid it with. In the left column after you've done that, you put "income." That's Roman numeral I. Roman numeral II is "savings." Just as the Bible says tithing is giving 10 %, it's arbitrary, but it makes the mathematics easy because all you have to do is move a decimal point. You want to pay yourself first, because if you wait until the end to pay yourself, there's never going to be any money. Uncle Sam takes out his income tax, the state takes out his income tax, and all those intangibles first, and you never miss it because you never see it. What you are going to do is tax yourself, just like Uncle Sam: state, federal, me (see financial chart). Take 10% off that and put it up in savings. That's Roman numeral II. Then the next thing you are going to have is "necessities," Roman numeral III. Necessities are what you cannot live without. A lot of people mix up wants and necessities because they want some things very, very badly. They put them in the necessities category, but they are not necessities. A necessity is what you have to have to live, to function: food, clothing, and shelter, for example. In a society such as the one we have, there are a lot of other things that at one time were not necessities, but they are now, such as the gas bill, electricity, car insurance, telephone, etc. Those are things that you really have to have in order to function. They go next. Then after that, you have what I call "installments." Installments should never run more than 10% of what you bring home either, to be safe. That gives you a little balance to buy "big ticket" items over a period of time. Then after that you get personal and other little things that usually run about 5%. Because you are starting out, your necessities are going to take up 65% of your income. In some instances, they will take up more; in some instances, less. These are just ball park figures. For a few months, it gives you a chance to see where your money is going. It gives you a systematic check on whether you're spending money on some things more than you should. It keeps you from being in denial (unconscious denial).

Another concept that we need to understand is "bring home" pay. What you make and what you bring home are different. What you earn total is gross, but all you can actually function with is what you're going to bring home. You have to find ways to minimize your taxes, but legal ways to pay

YOUR PERSONAL BEHAVIOR MAP TO SELF-FULFILLMENT

your fair share. You'll find that as you make more money, it takes more money. The best way to learn these concepts is to go to the literature that's available or go online and do research. You can buy software to do just about anything you want to do. Credit cards and credit limits are not recommended when you're just starting out, except for items that are necessary – not for ball games and other discretionary things – because credit cards are one of the biggest traps that young people can fall into. (People who are not so young fall into the credit card trap, as well!) These numbers can be tweaked, depending upon your particular situation. At the end of the page, you'll have totals: total owed, total paid, and total balance. I'm assuming that you're going to keep your job, or whatever your income is, for a reasonable amount of time. If you lose that job, you can get another one because you've been educationally sound and professionally sound. If you can readily assume that you're always going to have a pretty big salary for at least a year, at the end of the fiscal year you might get a raise or you might get cut, but you know what you've done for that year. Owning your own business is best, if you so desire. Not everyone will start in January. The corporation fiscal year is usually form July 1 to June 30, particularly for governments, business and colleges. Regardless of what period you started with, I suggest that in January, you look at what happened the year before.

    Look at your book and you'll get a pretty good

idea of your financial lifestyle. You find out that you might want to up it, or you might find that you have wasted funds that you should have done better with. When you start in January of that year, you should have some kind of idea or plan of what you're going to make, what you want to save, what you want to do, and where you going to go. At some point, you should start trying to save money for investing. Usually you don't want to invest until you have at least 6 months of money saved, so if something happens, you can live for 6 months without going up in smoke. Once you have that set aside, you can refer to any financial books to get started in investing. You can go to that web and find out a lot of things, too. All of the major brokerage houses have websites and publications to guide you. You can also get software that will show you how to do your financial planning and how to manage your investments. Most of the time, people don't want to follow the plan. They want to have what they want to have...Immediately.

Once you are working, you want to make sure that when you reach retirement age, you can live reasonably well for the rest of your life. It's important that you don't have "too much age at the end of the money." With the likelihood of Social Security downfall in the future, it is an individual's responsibility to take care of him or herself. The secret is to start at an early age, usually shortly after you first start working.

Financial advice for young people

I was fortunate to have started out teaching mathematics in high school in the mid 50's. Back then, I taught a course called general math, which was excellent because it dealt with all of the things students who were going to drop out of high school in grade 9 needed to know. (Back in the 50's, students didn't want to go past age 15 or 16 in school.) All of the basic, practical things that they needed to know were in that course. Young people who planned to go to college were jumping to take algebra, trigonometry, calculus and geometry, but I thought they should have had the basic course, too. It dealt with the American consumer. As I look back over the students I taught in high school, I find that a lot of them that didn't go to college are as financially sound as some of them that had gone to college. Both had problems if they never understood the American economy and the things that they should have done. The students who took the basic course were not considered very "academically skilled," but it was a great course and they really learned something practical. I learned some things when I taught it. By having taught it, I put it into practice. I found that the basic lesson of the course was that if you're going to live from month-to-month, you've got to be able to handle your finances. You're going to get old, so you might as well start investing at an early age. If you start early, it's like snowball going down the hill: it just gets larger and larger. After a while, you can't stop it. I have tried to teach that to my youngsters and my children, and they're pretty satisfied. They have portfolios of their own.

Many young people have an interest in being finically sound because they had grandparents living in their homes while they were growing up. A lot of them see that they're going to be in some serious situations. Youngsters have a keen sense of being able to project if you let them. If you can relate the material to where they are and what there're dealing with: if you ask them, "What if those things that you see are going to happen to you when you get to be 60?" They'll often say, "You know, Grandma and them are living with us. We have to take care of them." If you don't start at an early age putting money aside for you, then you're going to be in that situation, also.

I was introduced to financial concepts early

I was 11 when I started saving money. I had very good parents, and my mother and I had to fend for ourselves at an early age. My father was in the Navy for four years during World War II, and we didn't have extra funds to do a lot of things. This made me more financially responsible. When my father came home from the Navy, we had to live frugally because he was going to college on the GI Bill.

We had to manage our money very carefully, but it taught us a lot of things, and the things that they learned, I learned too. I was sort of like a brother, sister and a son to them because of my age and the fact that I was helping out so much. I was right there in the midst of it, and it truly helped me. My grandparents owned the corner store, farms and rental property. They always included me in their business because I was the oldest, and for a long time, the only grandson. My grandparents were getting old, so I helped out. I had a pretty good business mentality by the time I was in my early teens. I knew how to run a farm – we did tobacco, cotton, truck farming, the whole nine yards. I was not "directly involved" because I was the grandson, but I was around. I listened. I saw what went on. I helped to stock the grocery store shelves. I learned about credit early. I would come home in the afternoons and they would take a nap, and I would run the store. I would put the stock up. I would mark the prices. I would check everything out. I would put the bills up there.

My grandfather had a lot of those composition books where he had given people credit. My Granddaddy said to me, "Now you see those books up there?" I said, "Sure." He said " Well, those books are full of people owing me money. And I don't do any more credit business." He said, "Now they're going to see you in there and they're going to come down and want to get credit, and they'll think you don't know. They'll have all kinds of stories for you. Some of them will be true. We don't do any credit business because all you see in those books is money owed to me by some people in the neighborhood. If you look on the shelf, we pay cash for all that stuff when it comes in. If we don't sell something, we can eat it or use it up. It's yours. If you give it away to the people who say they're going to pay you, you're going to end up with some more books. Sometimes, I think if I might want to do that, I do that. You can't. you can't make these decisions."

He continued, "The second thing is everything that goes into the cash register does not belong to us. You'll see that there will be a lot of money in there, but you got to realize that the bills and taxes and things have to be paid for, so don't think we're getting rich by looking into the cash register. You got to keep the books, and then you will find where the money goes." My Granddaddy was also my Sunday school superintendent and that was at a time when I was the only grandson. Now, years later, I'm finding out that there's some type of biological attachments between grandparents and grandchildren. He would always say, "Where you want to go, boy?" I was like another son to him. I would ride in the back of the truck with him, and just had a marvelous childhood. I learned a lot, and the grown-ups didn't try to pull wool over my eyes. Whatever I wanted to talk about, that's what we talked about. I was never intimidated. There weren't any subjects that were off limits. Whatever I wanted to know about, we sat down and talked about. I'm realizing more and more how nice it was to have someone to talk about that in my life. I didn't realize back then, but I always been sort of a free spirit, and I've always been able to get past the thought police; I've always been able to think outside the box. Those attributes have helped me from a financial standpoint.

Wants versus needs: understanding what's important

My family was African-American, middle class. We always lived comfortably. In the late 40's and early 50's, after World War II, it was before television in small rooms and many people in small towns didn't have cars. The country was beginning to rebuild. My family had a car, we had a phone, and we had a house. My parents had jobs teaching school. We had income, and I never was hungry. I never had any kind of bad experiences. We were by no means wealthy, but I never felt deprived. I learned how to make decisions by what was necessary and what were wants by what was important. I knew there was going to be a paycheck every month. I knew that the bills were going to be paid and there was going to be food on the table. Basically, that's all I really needed. I had a basketball, and I didn't need all the other stuff.

I worked on the farms and in the summer, I went to Connecticut to live with some of my cousins. I got to know the North and I got to know the South. My cousins would come and spend time with me and we would work in tobacco and cotton, and we bought our clothes with the money we made.

I didn't experience racism personally. I knew

that it existed, but I lived in a black community and I knew where the white community was. The black and white kids would get together and play (until the white kids' parents would break us up). I didn't have "white friends." You just didn't go to their houses, but we played ball together secretly. When the parents didn't interfere, we had a great time. I had a good childhood. We knew what was going down, but it was just something that you didn't necessary talk about at that time. There were things that we didn't think were right, but we were not adults, so we didn't get into that.

Consider various time horizons when you plan

When you develop your financial plan, you need to set your immediate objectives, which cover now or the next week or so. Then you have short term objectives, which might covers a year or two, and then you have long term objectives, which might be from five to ten years. Then you have what I call very long term objectives, which is past that. Finally, I have added another category that I call financial objectives for eternity.

What are your financial plans for after you die? Seniors today have a tremendous amount of strength politically, because there are so many of them, and they've lived so long. They're more intelligent, because they have lived longer. Naturally, they want things to benefit them. I see in the future a sort of age war in which the seniors will want more and more things at the expense of the younger people who have to pay for those things. There are going to be more seniors and fewer young people, and mathematically, it's just not going to work.

This has increased the debate as to what to do with Social Security money. I'm not an economics expert, but I think young people should put some money aside for retirement and not rely on Social Security and Medicare alone to take care of them in their old age. There are two ways they can do this: they can put it aside from their jobs, because there are people who are in better shape to handle it and to invest it than they are; then some of the money that I said they were putting in savings, they should try to do something else with on the side, such as an IRA. I think that they should put away at least 10% of their earnings. Even the squirrels do that. That's your 10% savings. Pay yourself first.

A.G. Gaston was an Atlanta businessman who died a few years ago. He was written up in one of the first issues of *Ebony Magazine* in the 50's and I cut that article up and put it on the wall. He was a role model for me. One of the things he said in that article was pay yourself first. I never forgot that.

Think about retirement early

It's every individual's responsibility to take care of him or herself. I don't think that the natural order of things would have it such that somebody else will take care of you. You should do that yourself.

You've got the tools to do it. I hope the parents and teachers and other people who read this book will know that it is everybody's responsibility to start, at as early an age as possible, thinking about the time when they will not be able to work physically. If you're doing something you enjoy, you don't necessarily need to retire. Working keeps you young. It keeps the blood moving and the brain working. Many people don't feel good and they get diseases because they're not doing anything. They're bored, they're depressed, and they don't know it. That's because they're doing things that they don't enjoy doing.

Even if you stop working, you should have a hobby that you enjoy. The best situation is that you find a hobby that you love, and find a way and get paid for doing it. Once you are making enough money to live the way that you want to live, you'll be all right.

More is never enough

People think they need more, more, more. You have to learn how to master yourself. Find out what is important and what is not, and then just go with the flow. Don't even get on these stress tracks, because even if you are making an enormous amount of money, chances are you're under an enormous amount of stress. I've found out that they're directly proportional to each other. You're not going to make a lot of money unless you have a lot of responsibility. If you love it, fine; if you don't, then your aching for a stress attack.

This is an easy trap to fall into, because people go to college, they go to job training, and they get on track. Then they want to have big, beautiful homes, big, beautiful cars, all of those things. There's nothing wrong with that kind of lifestyle, as long as you are willing to pay the price that it's going to require from you. Usually when you're young, you have that energy. As you get older, you may feel that you don't want to do that as much. I'm not saying that you shouldn't have these things. They're great. Do not be a slave to your possessions.

Enlightenment means that you can live without any of the physical things that most people consider so important. There is a magazine called *Enlightenment* in which gurus, people who have supposedly found nirvana, are interviewed about their philosophies in life. I suggest that anyone who wants to find out about themselves and about the natural order of things and spirituality should read the magazine. It makes you internalize and think within yourself, and that's really where everything comes from. Nobody really has the answer. Anybody's answer is as good as anybody else's, if you actually believe it.

When you're in financial trouble

For people whose financial life needs some improvement, the first thing to do is to look at a financial notebook or your financial plan book.

Study it carefully (the money coming in and the bills you accumulated) in order to see your specific financial situation. The next step is to get some help. In larger cities, there is a program called "Consumer Credit Counseling Services" that is a health and human services program that is funded by federal, state and local governments.

You can go to them with all your bills and receipts and tell them, "I'm in bad shape." (This is not the same as filing bankruptcy or Chapter 11.) You can go to them anytime. They will look at what you have, appoint you a counselor, look at your books, and tell you what you need to do. The first thing they do is ask you for your credit cards. They say, in order for us to help you, you have to give up your credit cards. They have a big jar full of cut up credit cards. Then they figure out how much money you bring in and how much you need to live based on your bills. They come up with a plan for you. If you agree to that plan, they will call all your creditors. They will restructure your monthly payments to fit within your monthly income, and they will pay your bills for you. You have to give them a certified check when you get paid. It can't be late. When people approach me because they have gotten into a financial hole, I send them there to get straightened out. As long as you have a job and can make the payments, they will counsel you concerning things that you might have wanted in the past, but you really can't afford to have. You go in once a month to see how you are doing. You keep your same records (your financial book). Most of the time, people don't write things down, so they don't know, especially things that they don't want to know. I call this selective denial.

Budgeting itself is not that hard, but the idea may seem intimidating

I suggest that you use a cardboard box to keep your bills in. Some people pay bills weekly, some pay them at the first of the month. Usually if you make enough money, you pay them once a month because most of them come at the first of the month. If it comes at the first of the month, it's best to just list it, and you put it down, and you know where you are. It won't get lost because you know where it is. If you do the math, it's very simple. I've found that it's not that people don't know, it's that they really don't want to follow the math. Math has what we call a closer law, and that means two plus two is always going to be four. It's not going to be eight, like it or not.

Finance Course 101

1. You must have an income to match your lifestyle.
2. How much money you make largely determines your lifestyle.
3. Usually, you need a profession or a trade to ensure that you have a marketable skill.
4. Pay yourself first. That's what Uncle Sam does to your check.

5. Save a minimum of 10% of your bring home pay FIRST!
6. Live below your financial means.
7. Pay cash; it's cheaper.
8. Avoid the credit cards trap.
9. Keep some cash in your pockets at all times.
10. Don't try to be a fashion plate or clothes store.
11. You don't have to have the most expensive house or car.
12. Start slowly, study, learn, and find a proven, successful financial coach.

Some things to do

1. Make out your own financial plan in a spiral notebook (see sample financial plan in the quick-look section.
2. Follow your plan for at least six months, adjusting as you go.
3. Share your plan with your spouse or significant other. Include your children.
4. Go to the library. Talk with the librarians. Get online. Do research.
5. Find a good coach.
6. Do what you want to do.

Chapter 10

PROFESSIONALISM

What's the definition?

Webster's Dictionary defines profession as "A calling requiring specialized knowledge and often long preparation." I think people sometimes get jobs and professions confused. They don't have a clear definition of a profession or job. I think that a job is anything that you do to receive some type of monetary reward. It does not necessarily require that you train or have the skills, or even the interest for a long period of time. It's a paycheck. I think in this day and age, each person should be engaged in some type of profession, and I don't necessarily mean that you have to have long academic hours, or work yourself to death. Whatever you decide to do, there should be a legal and moral code for it, because there are some professions you can go into that are not in the best interest of society. We're talking about ones that there's a need for in society. You should prepare yourself for that at a very early age. That's where education comes in.

To choose a profession, you should find out what you really like doing best with a passion, and then get someone to pay you for doing it. If you can't get someone to pay you for doing it, find out how you can pay yourself for doing it. I can't make that point too strongly, because I've seen youngsters come to college, spend four years there, and not really know what they want to do.

Preparing young people for careers

When my students were working on their daily activities schedules, they also had to write out what they had planned to do (what they thought they wanted to do) for the rest of their lives. I taught them from freshmen to seniors, but I taught a lot of freshmen because I taught the freshmen wellness course. They were large, service classes that every freshman had to take. I didn't teach them all, but I had about two or three classes and I would have anywhere from 30 to 50 students per class. Most of them had no idea of what they wanted to do. It didn't really matter to me what they wanted to do, but they had to write down their career goals. Then they had to read them to the class, and we had a two minute question and answer period when the other students could ask why they wanted to do this. We already had information on their backgrounds because they had to write an autobiography for the class too, so we had a pretty good feel about who they were, where they came from, etc. The career discussion was to tell them where they were trying to go. Their daily activity schedule was trying to tell them how to get there. Once they did that, we had a student career center where students would go and access a big career data bank. They would type in what they wanted to do, what there major was, and it would print out for them what their career matches were. It was like a dictionary of occupational titles, and it would not only match up what they said they wanted to do, but it would also tell them what they should have in terms of education and preparation when they got ready to get the job.

When I teach my students about getting a job, I start from the job and go backwards. Most people want to go to school and then get a job. I suggest analyzing the job first and then come back to see what courses you're going to need to take the job. I ask them once you apply for the job, what are the skills you're going to need? They get the address and phone numbers, and they actually have to write that company a letter, tell them what their classification is, and that they want to come work with that firm. I also encourage summer employment where they are going, including co-op programs if they have them, because most of the students needed summer employment. In those programs, you work a semester. You're employed, you're in college, and you're learning a job. I take those letters up, and they get a grade for doing that. I say they have to send letters to three companies, no more than three. Then they find out what courses they need to take, what they need to have, what the job entails, and they get an idea also of what it's like going through the process of getting a job before they get to be a college senior. Most people think about what they're going to do at the end of four years. I spent four years and I really don't want to do this. So, by having that experience early, they had a chance to find out what it's like. I told them, now think about what you would like to do for the rest of your life, and then figure out how you can get paid for it. Most of them think about Hollywood, the NBA, NFL, being a hip-hop artist, about being on talk shows, or being star athletes or movie stars. I say, well there are a lot of things you can do based on your majors and what you want to do. You don't want to have to wake up every morning dreading to go to work, which so many Americans do. They were not taken through the process.

Applying the same concept to youngsters

Likewise, when we go out and work with the youngsters in the community, we're doing the same thing with them that I was doing with college students. It focuses them. It makes them think, I got to do something for the rest of my life. I say, well you guys want to drive these big pretty cars, and have the ladies looking at you, and wear your gold. Where are you going to get it? Selling crack is not an option, because that's a pretty hazardous job. First of all, you are either going to end up dead, a junkie, somebody's going to rob you, or you are going to get 20 to 50 years in jail. You can't do that for a lifetime. Don't even go there. Think about what kind of lifestyle you want to have, then think about how you're going to support it, then find out what you'd like to do to accomplish it. I tell them the process starts now. It starts today, and each day you build on, and build and build.

Then I put the letter K up on the board, which stands for *kaizen*. *Kaizen* is a Japanese word that means to continually get better. The Japanese always have that word around (*kaizen*) and I adopted it. There's another K word in the Greek called *kenosis* which means that you get rid of it. You houseclean. If things in your mind are not working, you've got to get rid of them. You've got to throw them away because, although they might have been good at one time, they serve no purpose now. Your brain is not necessary like a data bank, with limited amount of memory. It probably has infinite information storage capacity, but if you've got some clutter up in there, you just get rid of that.

"ICE" as it applies to the workplace

The educational process that I have called

"intergenerational collaborative enTergy" can apply to the workplace, as well. I believe that when you come on board in a corporation, there should be some connection for you all the way up to the president or the CEO, and that you should understand what they do. In most organizations, you don't know all the people who hired you. You're bought in to fix these little widgets, but how does the business process in this company works? Good companies should promote from within, in my opinion. Although someone starts at a lower level, you don't know what his ultimate potential is. You should let him know you have faith in him, teach him the ropes, and give him the opportunity in advance. His immediate boss has that primary responsibility, but there should also be someone above him or her, and so on up the line. It's like a chain. Every organization should want its employees to aspire to go on to the next level, and they should encourage it. If they develop this intergenerational collaborative "enTergy" in the workplace, then when the new employee comes in, he will know what's what. He will know that he may not make it all the way to the top, but he understands how the process works and it's available to everyone.

 I don't encourage gossiping from level to level in a job setting to impress, because when you do that, it can cause jealousy and envy among coworkers. Even if the rationale for that kind of behavior is explained, people feel threatened when it comes to their jobs and their livelihood. It's the responsibility of management to let all the workers know that they want everybody to do well, and they don't want anyone to feel threatened. People who invest in the company want the best possible employees they can have. If you look at it as lifelong processing, and lifelong education, you'll continue to grow, and they'll reward you accordingly.

Play to win

I guess that approach to work comes from being a coach. The only thing I know is we've got to start five people, and I'm going to start the best five I can get. Then I'm going to come back with the next best five. I've always had statistics and videotape to look at, and I always made evaluations every night. There are stories in the newspaper, on the radio, and TV every day. One thing about athletics: you get a report card immediately. That doesn't mean that I'm going to beg you to do this or that. I'm just going to let you know what the statistics are, and based on what they are, that's who's going to play. We all want to win. It's not about you and it's not about me. It's about the team. So let's go out and work hard, give our best. If we win, fine. If we don't, then we need to go back to the drawing board, because we're playing a win/lose game. Some people will tell you, it's not whether you win or lose. I say, if you show me somebody who doesn't care whether they win or lose, I'll show you a loser. T-E-A-M:

together everyone achieves more.

Commitment to community service starts early

When I taught school, I had class projects, and all of my classes had to do a minimum of ten hours of community work per semester. Right near the campus we had the Boys and Girls Club, and we had two recreation centers that we were in walking distance. I was on the board for most of those Boys and Girls Clubs for nearly 20 years, and I always worked with them in assigning students to work with the boys and girls. We devised some projects that could be done during spring and fall break. Sometimes the students had free hours, and they had to go over to the club and do some work. We came up with a program that had the youngsters working with the seniors. The kids in the Boys and Girls Clubs were youngsters. The recreation center was where the older people and parents went. We also had a program at St Augustine's University called community development resources in which college students worked with housing, physical fitness, and the whole nine yards. We have computers there and we structure after-school programs for the neighborhood kids and senior citizens who want to come and learn about computers. Most of our athletics majors know how to do this because they have to take computer sciences, so we get these students, many of them whom are world-class athletes, and the kids just gravitate to them. For example, when I introduce the kids to famous athletes, they're enthralled! The athletes talk to the youngsters about athletics, and they help them with their homework on the computers. The kids are so glad to be there with them.

Athletes as role models

You can do a lot of things with athletes that you can't do with other kids. When you expose youngsters to athletes they look up to, you get their attention. You start with sports and from sports, you explain how they have to get to high school first. Now, you have them motivated. Then you teach them some techniques on how they should run, play the game, skills, etc., how they should go to bed to early, how they should eat, and how they should stay out of trouble. They listen to you because they look up to you. Then they tell their parents about it. You say, "Tell your parents to come down with you the next time." I don't care where you go, most grandparents and parents are interested in their kids, and if you get the kids involved, you'll bring the adults into it. You say, "You come on down, too. We need you in this process too because you want them to be involved." Then the parents learn, too. A lot of people are just afraid to come to the place. The building just intimidates them. You get them there and you have punch and cookies, pizza, etc. and then you just sit down and talk. We try to get a high school athlete who's in the community to come there, too. Then your building this network, "ICE," and pretty soon you have a chain. Sometimes you have an overnight campout or picnic, or you'll go somewhere and play games. We may go down and have volleyball tournaments, softball games, track meets, and basketball tournaments on the campus. Then we see who can run the fastest so we find out who has natural talent. Everybody has a chance to participate.

I knew my passion early in life

I was in a great profession, and I tried to be good at it, all the way along. I got my first ball when I was 3 years old. The junior high boys and girls were having a tournament at school. At that time, we had what we called activity periods, and I was watching the game. There was a time out, and the ball was on the free throw line, so I ran out there on the floor and got it and went to the goal. It was the first time I ever had a ball in my hands, and I tried to shoot it. It caught on, and they threw me the ball. I tried to shoot it, again. I never did get it up that high, but when I came back I was smiling, and my mom said I had a great time. I played ball day and night; I had a little goal in my yard. I lived not too far from the schoolyard. I could run there. I had my ball and it just gave me great joy and pleasure. I played day and I played night. I just loved to play. Of course at that time, in the late 30's and early 40's, there was nothing else to do. There were no recreational centers; there were few TV's.

At that time, there wasn't even any African-American music that you could hear on the radio. You could buy it, but they didn't play it on the radio. So we played ball. We also had a little group of boys where you could go into the woods where we had a little camp. We'd sneak our mama's potato and meat – not enough so they would know some was missing. We build a log bridge, and we'd go swimming in the river. We had a great time as kids. We fished. We stayed gone most of the day. Our neighborhoods were safe. People didn't worry about where you were. They knew you were somewhere in the neighborhood and if you did something wrong, somebody was going to whip you and send you home and tell your mama, and then you'd get another whipping. Whoever got to the schoolyard first brought their ball, and you just started playing. Some kids had balls, some kids didn't. There was one guy who was an only child and he had everything he wanted. He was a spoiled brat. He'd bring his ball out there, and he wanted to play every game. When you lost, you were supposed to sit down, but you had to choose the next team. If he didn't get chosen, he'd say, "Give me my ball." Without him, there was no game. Once he was playing, all the calls went his way. We had to acquiesce because he had the ball and I used to just play and work on my moves and my game. I just loved it. I loved school back then.

Sometimes you change your mind

I graduated from school when I was 15. I was 2 years younger than most of the members of my class. I didn't think it would be in my best interest to skip any classes because I wanted to keep playing, and I knew if I went up I was going to be competing against people whom where more mature physically than I was. I was 14 when I got my college scholarship. We were playing Hillside in Durham in the tournament and I threw up 39 points, full court, 94/40, smoke and smother. I could run all night. I just didn't get tired. I could shut you down and keep running. If I got a shot, it never dawned on me that it might not go in. I just didn't miss. I got good grades, too, and I took a college prep curriculum.

I went to college and the medical doctor in town, who was a good friend of my parents, wanted me to be a doctor. They knew that they were going to need some doctors, and I didn't have any problems with that. My freshmen year I was majoring in pre-med, and I was playing ball at North Carolina Central. I found out when I got to college there were kids everywhere, and the academics and the athletes were a lot tougher than high school. I had to make a choice. If I was going to go to medical school, I was going to have to give up athletics. I really fell in love with athletics, so I majored in physical education and I had a minor in biology. That way when I got out, if I decided I wanted to be a doctor, I could take a couple of classes and get into medical school. I had a pretty heavy course load – trigonometry, calculus, and physics – and I was out there running too. I played under John McLendon, who was one of the greatest basketball minds in the world. We ran, ran, ran, ran and ran and when we went home at night, we didn't think about going out. There was only one place we could go, and that was bed. I was young then. I was 16 and I was running against guys who were 25 and 30, many of them World War II veterans (grown men who had families). Ultimately that got to be a bit much. They could do it, but I was still growing. Coach was very wise. He put freshmen together, and put them on a different floor from older guys. During that time in athletics, and given coach McLendon's values, the kids just didn't mess around. They didn't do drugs; they didn't drink; they didn't smoke. They kept your butt in line. It was a different breed of guys. They were clean-cut people, not only physically, but morally, too. None of that stuff went on because if they even caught anybody who thought that they wanted to get out of line, they'd whip their butts themselves. They were like big brothers. It was a different day.

When doors began to open

When I graduated in 1955, there were only two basketball players. A few years later, my college teammate Sam Jones played with the Celtics, Will Bill Russell and all those great championship teams. The first black athlete who went to the NBA from the CIAA was a player who played at North Carolina Central University – Harold Hunter. Earl Lloyd from West Virginia State was in there, too. There were some great players in the CIAA who later became NBA stars: Charles Oakley, Earl the Pearl Monroe, Sam Jones, Bobby Dandridge, etc.

Your career should be your passion

You should really love what you are doing, and you should want to do it, even without the money. Realistically, you've got to have food. You've got to support your family. We need to ask kids early on, what do you enjoy doing? We need to get them thinking about that, and then when it's time to choose a profession or career, they would have given it some thought. That doesn't mean every kid has to get an college education. He might want to be a computer repairperson. He might want to work with CP&L. Regardless of what it is, he should bring a passion to the table. I found something that I was passionate about, and I found out they would pay me for it. I would've coached for free. People talk about jobs, I figure I've had fun all my life. It was work, but it was work that I enjoyed doing. The hours that a coach puts in are long, intense and rough, and I think that anybody should approach his profession or his job this way. My whole life has been consumed with my family, teaching and athletics, I guess mainly because I came from a family that taught. I helped mom and dad correct papers when I was young. I enjoyed teaching and coaching. Then I became an athletic director because after I started working, I found out that, basketball, if the football coach was athletic director, the football team would have spent the money by the time my turn came around. So on my second job, I made sure that wherever I went, I was also athletic director. I tried to be fair to all the sports, because I had been in the other position. I tried to have enough resources for everybody.

BUPDL Leadership

When we used to have coaches meetings, I'd always be in what I call "bottoms up participatory democratic leadership" mode. I would always give all the coaches a little checklist as to what their problems were. They were supposed to find out those problems from the players and themselves. Then were they not only to put the problem down succinctly, but then each coach was supposed to develop his or her solution to it along with where the money was coming from. At athletic directors meetings, we'd start the year off discussing the main problems. Sometimes we would have the athletes, but the money wasn't there. We'd list the top five problems in order of importance (hierarchy). Then we would list whether we had some possible solutions. Then we would ask, can we handle the problem? What do we think is required to handle it? If we can't do it ourselves, what do we think administration should do? Then we would estimate the cost and talk about how we would raise the money. When you asked them how to raise the money, that eliminated a lot of things, so it got to the stage in process where you pretty much knew they needed it. Then once they did that a lot of times, you could get fundraising ideas from other coaches. Then I would go to the corporate community for certain things to get funds, too. There were alumni I could call and say, "You know we need this," or there were foundations. That gave me a way of letting them know, and usually I didn't go past the first two for all of them. Then I would get that together and take it to the administrators, and then I had a rationale for it. I would explain that this came from the players, or the coaches, as the case would be. The things I could resolve with coaches, I did. The things that I couldn't resolve with them, I took to the administrators and asked for help.

Know when it's time to leave

A coach's life is not 8 to 5. A coach's life is total commitment: 24-7-365. Once I reached the point that I didn't feel like total commitment, I just resigned. I knew it was time...you can feel it coming. The game is a great game. It's been too good to me to do less than my best. I could never do that. I wasn't raised that way. I said I've enjoyed it but I don't think I can commit to the hours, the time, and the energy that are needed to keep it at the level where I have brought it to any longer. My body is telling me I need to slow down. I can't work those 18 and 20 hour days, day in and day out. I resigned at the tournament game. 14,000 people were there. I hadn't told anybody, except my wife, in advance. When I was sitting on the bench, I knew I didn't want to sit there anymore. At the end of the game, I got the mic, and I said I would like to make an announcement. We had gotten barbecued. It happened because I was getting ready to build another championship team. The school had run into some financial problems and they cut the budget by 30% and increased tuition by 20%, which meant I had a 50% loss in my budget. I couldn't continue to give the scholarships like I had and recruit like I had, and it was showing. That year, I didn't recruit any new people except an all-star junior college team. Junior college kids usually need to play for three years. You don't want them to play the first year because they have to get acclimated. They think they can play, but they're playing on a junior college level. when you get to a four year college, it's a lot different. I had the best we could get, and I sat them out, and let them be the scout team. They were going to be the other folk's team when we practiced, but the public didn't know that. That's where most of the scholarship dollars had gone. It's like they say, you get what you pay for. I was playing primarily with the students who were graduating and who had come to school as physical education majors but who hadn't made the team, so that I could have scholarship money for the next year.

Two years after I left, the succeeding coach won the CIAA Tournament Championship. He was a good coach and a personal friend of mine. At the end of my last tournament, I said, "I just want to let you all know that this is my last game. I am retiring as of this game. I want to apologize for the way we played today," I said, "Because we didn't play well. It's been a good 30 years. I have enjoyed it, and you've been wonderful. I just want you to be the first to know." They stood up, 14,000 people, and they gave me a standing ovation. I walked on into the sunset. I choked up later, but I was in control that night. I knew it was the right time. The story was all over the 6 o'clock news.

Money talks: athletics in the segregated South

Back in the 60's and the 70's, there were a lot of great black ball players in African-American colleges. African-American colleges were the place to be for athletics at that time. Caucasians would go and see the African-American teams play, and on New Year's Day when they had the bowl games, the white southern teams who had great records were getting barbecued – Bear Bryant at Alabama, and all those schools. They had no African-American ball players. The reason that they had records was because they hadn't played the top teams. That was hype, because you were living in that time and it just wasn't accepted. The black players who could play went to the Midwest, the West coast, and Syracuse. They were recruiting these players from the South, but you never heard about them until there were bowl games, because TV games weren't that prevalent, either. The only games you really saw were local games and then the bowl games because they were carried by the big networks. People would say, well here's Bobby Bell from New Bern, North Carolina, and folks went, what in the world's he doing out there?

There was a whole lot of money going around, and where they were playing, the teams were making money. So they found out that, if we don't have some African-American ball players, folks wouldn't want to see us play. You're talking about money. Money's green. Everybody understands money. That means it happened. When it happened in the public schools, there was a lot of money to be made, too. Everybody was playing and at that time there wasn't too much you could go see. Everybody loved to go see the athletics teams. The gym would just be overflowing. When they first integrated the schools, they still had racially separate schools. The African-American students who wanted to go to the Caucasian schools could go. The feeling was that there was going to be a big bonanza because the Caucasian schools in the South had never played African-American schools. They had always been separate. The Caucasian press played up how the African-American teams were going to get barbecued by the other teams, because that's all they had scooted or seen. They didn't know anything else. Then they started playing, and they started to have to play 84/32. It was an altogether ball game. After integration, they took the best African-American ball players, the best teachers, and the best students and put them in the all-Caucasian schools. That left most of the African-American schools at a pretty big disadvantage because Caucasian students didn't enroll in public African-American schools, but we knew that. That's when I retired from high school coaching and went to college. I couldn't continue to field the teams that I had been filling with all my players gone.

    I coached at the high school level for 16 years and college for 25 years. When I first graduated from college, I coach high school in Clayton. I won the state championship there. The first year I coached in Gatesville County, we won a championship there. I really loved Clayton, because that was my home, and I knew the kids, their parents, the town folks, and for Clayton to win the state championship, it was totally unheard of. Not only did I coach the kids, but I also taught them. They all had to take my classes, which at the time were algebra, geometry, physics, chemistry, physical education and biology. You had to teach everything back then, because at that time there weren't a whole lot of teachers. I taught Sunday school; I was assistant superintendent, and my father was superintendent of Sunday school, so I had them in church, too. I had them pretty much all the time. One mama said if Coach Heartley would tell them to go run into that wall, they would go and do it. I enjoyed them. I played with them, because at that time, I was still playing. I could show them what to do. You know it wasn't a matter of saying it. I could just get out there with you and demonstrate.

My own career saga

When I graduated, I was drafted by the Minneapolis Lakers of the NBA (they're the Los Angeles Lakers now), but they didn't know I was black. They thought I was white. NCCU-NCSU-UNC were often misrepresented. There was no elaborate scouting system for the NBA. We're talking the 50's now; the war was just over. They had to just listen and see what things were. We had write ups in the paper, just like Duke and Carolina College. A lot of them thought it was Carolina College, and a lot of them thought it was Carolina or Carolina State. I had good stats, so I was drafted. I didn't even have the money to go to Minneapolis, and besides, that, it was cold. I didn't want to go. I was working in New York with the City of New York as a Physical Activity Director, and I enjoyed that, but I wanted to coach. I had two contracts to coach in North Carolina. I didn't want my kids to grow up in New York. I wanted them to grow up in my home and with my grandparents. I left New York and came to Gatesville, NC. I stayed there for a year, then I came to Clayton. I stayed there for about 7 years, built a great program, enjoyed all of it. That was during the time integration was really out and Raleigh had a better school system. I thought about the education of my kids. People had wanted me to come to Raleigh, but my kids were not school aged at that time. Then they passed school age and I moved to Raleigh, and went on at high school there, which was a very good high school (Ligon High School). I worked there from 1964 to 1970. Twiggy Sanders, who played with the Harlem Globetrotters, went there. I gave him his first basketball. I had some great years, some championship years. I coached football, basketball, and tennis. I had four state tennis championships, both men and women. After integration, I started losing players. I went into state government because at that time they were having problems in the school system with the African-American kids and Caucasian kids fighting. Terry Sanford was governor, and he said he needed somebody who was respected and that the people in the community knew to negotiate racial issues. This was in the early 70's. The racial tension was spreading out everywhere in North Carolina. So we developed a youth coordinator. Then, after some success, they made me the district coordinator for the fifth congressional district from Virginia, all the way to Florida, to Tennessee. I went to the CIAA tournament, and they were bouncing that ball, and I decided to come back. Everybody said, "Why don't you come back? We need you." In Raleigh, their colleges weren't doing too well, so they wanted me to come back. That's how I got back into coaching. At Christmas my first year, we were undefeated. I had some veterans and some pretty good players, and we did well. My first mistake was when I went to recruit. I didn't recruit kids that were big enough or fast enough to be in the college area. I didn't know too much outside of North Carolina, so as far as recruiting, and I tried to recruit in North Carolina. Then I found out I had to compete with State, Duke, and Carolina. All those kids that I'd coached against! I knew they weren't thinking about coming to St. Augustine's. That reality hit me. They were bigger, they were faster, they were stronger. It takes you a couple of years to find that out. You might have been alright in high school son, but they'll eat you alive in college. You have advisors when you go to college. Once you get there and you register, you think you know what you want to do...then some of you don't. Those that don't go to an undeclared advisor, who are usually at the student development center. What they do is advise those students who haven't decided what they want to be. What I tried to do with the athletes that I brought in, for those who didn't know what they wanted to do, was persuade them to go into physical education, whether they wanted to be teachers, whether they wanted to go pro, whether they wanted to do physical therapy, or whether they wanted to work with handicapped people. There were a whole lot of things you could do. The reason I did that was because I wanted to teach them, because I wanted to relate with athletes with what was going on in the classroom. Also, it let me keep an eye on them in class.

Career change

In this time of rapid change, your career might change two or three times, or you might get tired of what you are doing. Unless you save a lot of money, you have to do something else, so whatever it is that you've developed an interest in, you start to work on that and develop your skills later. Then you make the jump. It might just be that you are going to move to another level in the same profession. Rather than being a teacher, you are going to be, say, a supervisor. After you become a supervisor, you might want to be a superintendent. You might want to get out the field and go into counseling. There are so many things that you might want to do, but you don't need to change until you thought about it for a while. You always really need to look at the pluses and the minuses. You also need to talk to people who are in the field, because there are a lot of caveats that exist out there that you don't see.

Motivated by money

If a kid tells me he want to make a lot of money, I say, "Who makes a lot of money?" There's nothing wrong with making a lot of money. Money is great, great medicine for most ills. Everybody should

YOUR PERSONAL BEHAVIOR MAP TO SELF-FULFILLMENT

make as much money as they possibly can make. Then you have to learn how to make money. I think it's an admirable goal for people to want to make money. We've made money a bad thing. Most of the people I know that have money do good things. Most of the people doing bad things are the folks trying to make money. Going back to my philosophy on how to choose a profession, you find out what you really like to do and get paid for it – for yourself, then others second. If you can't get paid for what you really want to do, then you have to do what I call thrift thinking. You have to think, I'd really like to do this, but I don't think I can make enough money at it. If you think about it, if you're really good at what you do, you can make a lot of money. I don't care what it is. If you're the garbage man, if you're a good garbage man, people will pay you to come get their garbage and keep it like it ought to be. I'll just take Tiger Woods, for example. All he does is hit the golf ball. You can make a hundred million dollars hitting a golf ball? Now that's probably a little bit way out, but all I'm saying is if you really like it and you're good at it, you can make just as much money as you need. When I say as much as you need, I don't mean as much as you want, but enough to carry your lifestyle. Anytime you have enough money to live without having to work, you're rich. You can't ever get enough to do everything you want, but you can get enough. I will still say do what you want to do with a passion, and get paid. If you can't do that, then find out what you can get paid and stay in that job long enough to put yourself in a situation where you don't have to do it again if you don't like it. I think the bottom line is: if you really want to do something, if you are going to get paid for it, you can be whatever you are willing to work to be.

Some things to do

1. Write out honestly what profession it is that you would like to pursue.
2. Write out the assets and skills you possess that would make you a success in that profession.
3. Seek the advice of a successful person.
4. Write a plan for pursuing your professional choice or choices.
5. Go to the library. Talk with the librarians. Go on-line. Do research.
6. Find a good coach.
7. Do what you want to do.

CHAPTER 11

POLITICS

Define it first

According to *Webster's Dictionary*, politics are "The art of guiding and influencing policies." Of course, you are never supposed to use the word to define itself. I look at it as competition between people, groups, or individuals for power, control and leadership. Politics started with Adam, Eve and the serpent in negotiation of the apple, if you believe in that story. There were three beings vying for power, control and leadership. God supposedly gave the power to Adam and the job of following to Eve. If you have a leader, you also have to have followers. In any political relationship, you have to answer this question: who's going to do the leading and who's going to do the following?

Politics at home

Politics start in the home, between husband and wife in deciding who wants to assume leadership, the power, the control. We're going through some trying times now, because in the Southern Baptist Church, in the Muslim religion, and a lot of other man/wife religious situations, we're trying to say that men have certain place and women have certain place. I think people do have places. It doesn't matter whether you're a man or a woman. If were trying to do what's best for the body politic, then the leadership will depend on who can get the goals accomplished, be they male or female. Because traditionally men have been the leaders, they often assume they have all it takes to be a leader, and that is questionable. When I taught mathematics and other courses that were analytical, the women were often way ahead of the men, but sometimes they would not let on. When I read papers and corrected them, though, I knew who knew what was going on, and I encouraged them. Even way back in the 50's, I told them that there's no corner on mentality, there's no corner on brains. I read the book, *Men are From Mars, Women are from Venus*, and I'm happy to say that we never had those problems because we had an egalitarian family. My mom and father ruled together. If there were conflicts, my mom would defer to my father. Not necessary that she thought that he had more sense, but because we were bought up in a traditional Christian family, and my grandparents were of the opinion that a man ruled the house. The women had input, but if it came down to one person's way, it usually was the man's way. He had a responsibility then, because if it broke down, that was the problem, with choices and consequences. If we go with your choice, you deal with the consequences. They usually talked things out. Not only do you have the politics going on between the adults, but the children also act politically because they try from day to day to manipulate the parents. They'll cry. They'll want to be picked up. We had a rule in our house that if a child was well, didn't have a temperature, was dry and fed, we let him or her cry. It helps develop their lungs and vocal cords. Parents need to have some strategy like that because children will learn how to manipulate you by figuring out what makes you vulnerable. Whether you think you're in the political arena or not, you're in one, and it starts at home. You need to be aware.

Community politics

If you aren't careful, you'll be persuaded by the thought of the people in the community, because they want you to do what they want you to do. They will control your mind, too. If you don't go along with them, they will put sanctions on you to let you know that your thoughts are not the thoughts of the group. You have to be careful about that. So what you have to know is: how do I act? What type of leadership do I want to bring to the table? Do I want to lead or do I want to follow? I find the people who want to lead are not the people who should be doing the leading. Often the people who are following are doing so because they have looked a step beyond where the ones that want to lead are, and they don't think that, in the long run, they want to put up with all the issues that are out there. I think that politics in themselves are a very noble profession. I was in politics for one year, and I knew that I was not going to make a very good politician. I could have if I wanted to compromise some of my integrity, and if I wanted to let my ego get the better of me. I just didn't think that compromising my integrity was good for me.

<u>Making a difference as an individual</u>

To live our political lives effectively, we need to be productive and help influence the family, the community, the faith community, our businesses, or corporations, and our political parties. We need to be able to bring something to the table, and usually that means some time, energy, money, skills, and other resources like facilities. Those are things that you look at when you bring help to a political arena. Often people don't know what they bring to the table. If we're going to prepare the table such that everybody is going to eat, then somebody has to prepare the food. If you're eating, at some point you need to bring something of value to the table. You can't just always pull your chair up. That's the way I used to talk to my basketball teams: "Son you know, we want you to play, but you've got to bring something to the table. You know you have to make a contribution."

In the community, we speak of civic responsibility. Most of the time when people think about politics, they think about the Democratic Party and the Republican Party, who's mayor, etc. but if we think about doing something to help people, then we become in essence mini-leaders ourselves by realizing that we have a responsibility to do something.

I was listening to the presidential debates last year, and the morning after the debate, I heard Tom Joyner do a critique of it. *The Tom Joyner* show is nationally syndicated FM radio show with a primary African-American listening audience. That morning, Tom said, "Neither one of the guys touched on any of the black issues. What about HIV/AIDS? What about inner city growth? What about affirmative action?" He pointed out strongly that African-American people had an agenda too, and he had Al Gore on the phone the next night. Tom Joyner has substantial influence with African-American voters, so he's going to be a factor in the political arena. Then I take it a step further. I say if we know what's important and what needs to be done, then why don't we do it? If these are the things that affect us, then certainly the government should help. They have resources, too. When I say "we," I'm not necessary talking about African-American people, Caucasian people, Asian people, etc. I say we're all people. Your problem is my problem and my problem is your problem. Most people don't look down the line and anticipate the natural order of things. If it's going to affect me, eventually it's going to affect you. I need to get it straight with you before it jumps over to me. That's what happened with Hitler and Milesovic, and all those people who let others take advantage of them without anybody saying anything and doing something about it. If they take advantage of you, they'll take advantage of me, and vice versa. You have to look at it from that standpoint.

Political parties

I've been a Democrat for a long time, and I probably will continue to be one because I think that it has shown that it's the best party for those people who are concerned about the majority of people. I have nothing against the Republican Party, if they have ideas and actions that respond to issues affecting the majority of the people.

There's always going to be a problem between Republicans and Democrats, because there's always going to be differences among people on many fronts. The things that rich people want are not going to be the same things that poor people want, but I think there has to be a happy medium in there somewhere. Bush talked about big tax cuts. Gore said Bush was going to give it to the rich people. I think somewhere down the line, the rich people ought to get some money, and the poor people too. It doesn't have to be a either or scenario. I always say it's either/or/and. It took me a long time to learn that you don't have to choose one or the other; often you have both. That's the paradox of living. In some instances, the two sides look like they're diametrically opposed, but in reality, they're not. A good leader is one who is able to identify some core things that would be fair to the rich, some to the middle class, some to the poor, and what's ultimately going to be best for the people most of the time.

Politics in the church

As of the writing of this book, there is a spilt political in the church. The Southern Baptists are stating that they don't necessarily want a woman in the pulpit, and that the duty of the wife is to follow the husband. I don't have any problems with that if that's the way they want it, but from an egalitarian standpoint, I don't think it's a good idea. I've known a lot of women with much more ability and a lot more skills then most men, and that's a big source of problems that have come up within the churches and the organizations. As I have taught relationships in college, I have got a pretty good idea in what a male wants and what a female wants, and usually they're not too different. In class, I made the males take the female's role, and the females take the male roles in roll-playing scenarios. It got uncomfortable because they had to try to prove a situation that they were not necessary in agreement with. That's when their feelings would come in. Logic is one thing, but emotions are something else.

Social habits are also a strong influence on people. When you put somebody in another situation and say now you got to argue the ladies' side, they say, what do you mean? Both genders usually struggle with the exercise. Eventually everybody gets a better view and a better grasp of how everybody feels, and oftentimes how selfish their own desires are. In the Muslim faith, women cannot do certain things. In fact, I don't know of any religion where women are in charge and they tell the men that they can't do certain things. There might be one, but I don't know of any.

I believe in politics that exist between individuals should be the same politics that exist within the organization. In business, women make only about 75% of the money that men make, and there are glass ceilings that prevent them from getting the highest-level positions. I think all that should change, but I'm not in that area. I know that some men have a difficult time taking orders from women. Why, I don't know, but they do. I've seen it in organizations. The mere fact that the women is running something, all of a sudden she isn't qualified in eyes of men, even if she's got a PhD in Administration. She's working for the corporation, so what do you mean she can't run it? We have to break those walls down.

Politic defined by culture

Certain beliefs are instilled in you because you have to take on the beliefs in which you live. Perhaps the culture in which you live says that this is a man's world, and believe that, but America was settled and developed by both men and women. The reason that women have the freedom in America as they do is because they were out there defending their families, cutting trees down, and growing food, too. They have just as much right as men do, if you just think about it. They don't want to be bothered by the facts and the truth; they just want what they want. When you sit down and look at the literature, you have to realize that sometimes the literature is biased, too. So when you look, you have to look at all of the literature, not just selected literature. I wouldn't say that text books are necessary inaccurate, but they give you a frame of reference.

History is just what it says: His-story." You can't prove most of it. The Bible assembled as one book hundreds of years after Christ. Most people can't remember what happened last year. Can you image trying to form a book hundreds of years after the event happened? Then again, the Bible is a history of Jewish leaders and their people. It isn't history of all mankind. The world was still going on. Most of the time it was the leaders, the kings, the scribes, the lawyers, those people who wrote books, so you have to look at everything within the context of how things were at that time.

Lessons about politics

My overall message to readers is that, in every aspect of your life, you've got to know that politics exist. You need to get involved and make a difference; you need to make sure you do not compromise your integrity. There are two things that you don't want to do: compromise your integrity and let your ego get out of control. I found that sometimes people get into positions of leadership because they want all the prestige and perks that go with the job. Then when they get there, I find that a lot of them get into what I call the leadership trap. They realize that it's not really what they want to do, but people want them to continue. They want you to do all the work and solve all the problems, and if it doesn't work then they'll say, see, I knew he wasn't the right leader to start with. Now you are talking politics. The political arena can make some people intoxicated with power. They have the people, the tax base, money and other resources. They have the approval of at least one group, and once they get in there, they just don't want to leave. The first Continental Congress was not that way. We were supposed to go there in the spring, have a little meeting, find out what was going on, what was needed, make appropriations, and then go back home. Then they started raising taxes and they got Washington, DC laid out. It got to be nice, and they said, "Hey, I could get used to this!" It's intoxicating. Once they get in, they don't want to leave. I'm not saying that you have to leave, or that getting intoxicated with it is bad. I think it's bad if you're not doing the will of the people.

Developing future leaders

I think there should be time limits on all positions of power because, although you might be doing a great job, the purpose of the leader should develop competent followers who will eventually replace you. Most people want to lead and keep everybody else down, but my true definition of a leader is one who develops future leaders along the way. As a teacher I didn't just want to develop followers of just college graduates. I was trying to develop leaders. I tired to develop all my students as leaders. I knew all of them were not going to be leaders, but they had to be subject to the leadership atmosphere to find out what it was about so they would have a better appreciation of the people who did lead. You'll be a better follower if you tired to be a leader, if that's what you wanted to do.

"BUPDL" leadership

There are a number of different leadership styles: autocratic, democratic, monocratic, laissez-faire, etc. mine is what I call BUPDL: Bottom up, Participatory Democratic Leadership. It's the method that gives everybody in the group the responsibility to bring something to the table. Some people are going to bring more than others, but the group decides for the group what's the best thing. It doesn't mean yours was bad. We've got a record of it because although it might not be good now, two or three years from now, it might be pertinent. We know where it is.

I think it's sad that we only have two candidates that people say are able to lead the country. I know that's not true. You've got to raise one hundred million dollars to be president. I don't know how you're going to get around money. Money is a hard thing to get around, in politics or any other aspects of life. Normally the more money that goes to an aspect of living, the better it gets. If the plan was a good one, the better your life processing will be, all things being equal. Money is simple stored work. If you got money in the bank, you had to get that money some kind of way, most likely through some type of work. Then you store it (save and invest it) so that you could reuse it. There's a book called *The Psychology of Money* that I would recommend to readers. It shows how people react to money and how certain things are processed psychologically because of money. There's also a book called *Sexual Politics* that deal with politics of gender, and because you got men and women who are always in some type of political situation, you need to be aware of it to know if it's being used on you. You could go to any good library or internet and find material on politics. If you really want to do something, you can do it. It's just a matter of doing it. Just be what you want to be. Behave that way.

Some things to do

1. Get yourself and all your family members that are 18 years and older, and register to vote.
2. Schedule a meeting with your voter precinct chairperson.
3. Attend the next precinct meeting with your eligible family members.
4. Volunteer to become a block chairperson.
5. Register with political parties of choice.
6. Go to the library. Talk with the librarians. Get online. Do research.
7. Find a good coach.
8. Do what you want to do.

HARVEY D. HEARTLEY, SR.

Chapter 12

SEXUALITY

What do you mean?

Without sexuality, the human race or any species would cease to exist. *Webster's Dictionary* defines sexuality as "Relating to or involving sex, or sexes." When I use the term sexuality, I want to include sensuality also. To be sensual means the gratification of the senses or sex. So when we say a person is sexual, we're not necessary saying that that person is sensual.

We are all sexual beings. We manifest our sexuality in different ways, but we're born male or female biologically. That's what I call the plumbing, the equipment. How we are raised determines our gender because, although you may have been born a male, you may have female tendencies. Although you may have been born a female, you might have male tendencies. From biological standpoint, until the first six weeks in the development of the fetus, everybody is thought to be female. Whether the sex cells develop into testes depends upon a hormonal make up of testosterone and estrogen and the other sex hormones that determine what you're going to be. From the standpoint of men who are gay, there could be a biological explanation having to do with the sex hormones. Whether you are male or female is decided within your brain. The brain has to make that decision as to what you are (these are my theories). It might happen that the signal is sent to the chromosome or the genes for you to have the sex organs of a male, but in the brain (due to hormonal mix-up or faulty chemical imbalances) it's determined or deciphered as female. This means that there is possibly a biological error that explains why a man can be gay. A female is a little bit different because all females who are born females are always going to have the sexual organs of a female. They are never going to develop a penis. In my mind, in the brain, the brain chemistry might just secrete or give the genes the recognition that you're a male, but the equipment is female.

We see aberrations in everything. Things change. All trees are not the same trees, all squirrels are not the same squirrels. It's clear that nature makes mistakes also, and that's when we get into some situations wherein people may not know whether they are male or female. I think parents should know these things, and so should the faith communities. I don't think we should make judgements about people sexuality. These things start at an early age because youngsters will explore their genitalia, often we will slap them on the hand and admonish them when they don't know what they are doing. They do that because research shows it's pleasurable and they're exploring (unknowingly) their sexuality. Somewhere in their life it's developing their sexuality, and we shouldn't be unduly concerned about that.

The responsibility of parenthood

When you bring somebody into the world, you have to think about the fact that you're going to be his or her parents forever. That concept might be a little foreign to people, and might be a little bit way out. A young parent may say, when he gets to be 18...I'll be so glad when he gets to be 18, but that's not the point. The philosophy of parenthood is that you bring somebody into the world that you might have to take care of for life because he or she might be born with a disability or a defect. Don't think that you're going to be absolved of your parental responsibility when they turn 18. You're their parents for as long as they live, and as long as you can help them, I think you have moral obligations to do so. Your responsibility never ends. We need to be very careful about bringing youngsters into the world. To ensure that they maintain good health, you need to look at prevention, education, treatment and rehabilitation. The first aspect to address is the unknown prevention. You need to know what's going on in the sexual area. You also need to know what will be going on when you decide to have sex with someone, and what age that should happen. When youngsters reach the age of puberty, they should know about it. The parents should know about it. In some states parents, have to decide if some students get sexual education in school, or not. It's not taught as a basic subject, but children can take it ex officio if their parents sign a statement. In reality, it's the parents sometimes who aren't comfortable and who probably aren't doing a good job talking about it at home.

Most churches don't want to talk about it, either. Sex and procreation are at the base of all life. You cannot skirt around that. As a parent, you have to sit down with your children and talk about it. Not only that, you have to know what you are talking about. Questions are going to come up, so you need to know beforehand what the questions are and what the answers are. The answers come from literature, the experts, and the faith community. They also come from your faith; the two are not contradictory. It's not by accident that human nature has made it possible for the human race to reproduce at very early ages: 10, 11, 12. The reason for that is that in an agricultural agrarian economy, we need as many people to till the land and share the work responsibility as possible. When I was talking about creativity and imagination to us, but in the grand scheme of things, He thought it was in the best interest of man to be able to reproduce at an early age. God gave us choices; He didn't give us answers. If you go back to the natural order of things (N.O.O.T.) and the way that we live in the past, the children came up within a social community, waiting for somebody to teach them. The best people prepared to teach the youngsters how to live are the grandparents and elders. The young people, the parents at that age, don't know how children should be raised. The only thing they knew was to how to have them. They needed to work and help provide for the elderly people who no longer may be able to do physical work. We have choices, and society has decided that young people shouldn't have sex because it creates too many problems: social problems, emotional problems, sexually transmitted disease problems, etc. Yes, that's true. But the body says it wants sex, so you've got a conflict. Remember that life is a paradox. In infinite wisdom, we have to figure out a way that is best for us. What works best for the community? Is ignorance of sexual matters best, or is intelligent best? Inasmuch as God gave everybody the right to choose, you can't protect the kids forever. You have to let them know the facts of life. You have to let them know where you stand. Let them know what you think is in their best interest and the community, and then the choice is left to them. In case of err, they should know what safe sex means. I believe we should teach young people about contraceptive products (birth control pills, condoms, etc.), all of the things that will keep them from getting into situations we know they can't handle. As parents, we should let them know the psychological effects of early sex. Not necessarily morality implications, but when you been intimate with another person, there are certain spiritual and emotional feelings that are going to exist. They won't necessarily exist forever, but we know biologically that they will exist for a while. Then after that, it dwindles, and for each little passage that you go through, the sexuality and the sensuality change. Over time, the endorphins are not jumping up and down like they were in the beginning. That kind of romantic love is not going to last forever. As you grow through your 20's, 30's, 40's 50's, 60's, 70's, and 80's, certain things are going to happen to you sexually and each other aspect of life. You will know that these things will occur beforehand and make plans for the time they arrive.

Sexual politics

Sexual politics means that some people will use sex to get their way. You have to be aware of that because it exists in the family between husband and wife. There are certain roles that men think wives should play, and there are certain roles that wives think that men should play. You can go to the lecture and see what the majority of people think, which doesn't really mean anything, but a least you know the mindset of the community and the environment. You really have to sit down and talk that situation out with your spouse or significant other. You have to be open about those things because your philosophy might diametrically be opposed to that of the other person.

Some people are just sensual by nature. They're easy going, they're easy to get along with, and there's just something about them that seems to attract people. They don't necessary have to be beautiful or rich, but they have something that we call class. Class is not the school you went to. It's not the car you drive, it's not the clothes you wear. Class either is or isn't. You can't buy it. Class is simply is. People with class don't have to say anything. They don't have to come in wearing a mink coat, but there's always a presence when they are around, an aura. It makes you just smile to yourself.

Sexual philosophy

There are basically 4 primary reasons for sex: sex for pleasure, sex for procreation, sex for money, and sex for political reasons. I've found out in my life that men and women have sex for different reasons. Most men have sex because they were biologically predisposed to have sex. The more women that men had sex with and had children with, the more their genes are dispersed. From this, we would have a wider variety of people, with, hopefully, different positive traits. Testosterone is more prevalent in men than women. Most men have sex and then fall in love after the fact. Most women fall in love first and then have sex.

I think that women are by nature predisposed to look for a man who can protect and provide for them and their children, because biologically they know there's going to be a time when they can't provide for themselves (during pregnancy and immediately after childbirth). Over the years, nature and evolution have said to the woman, before you can go out here and try to have pleasure, you have to think about whether you can survive, and whether your offspring are going to survive. Women will delay and try to find those traits in a man that they can feel comfortable with, and feel belonging to, and being cared for, because eventually they're going to have sex. We had no birth control products in the natural order of things (N.O.O.T.). Through the years, they have been developed and they enable women to look around until they find someone they really like, someone they are comfortable with and they believe will take good care of them and their children. They then decide they love him and are ready to have kids.

In recent years, we have been biologically predisposed in a different manner. Society says its best for you to have 1 spouse or 1 mate. That's in the western world. In some countries, a man can have up to 4 wives, legally, if he can support them, and there's an order to that. In America, we said you can't do that. What you have are married men who might have mistresses, and wives who want to hold their husbands to their wedding vows, and it's embarrassing if that doesn't happen. We have to think about those things, too. There again, it's in the contract that exists between the consenting people. We don't have answers; we have choices, and all choices are paradoxical; consequences follow choices. Every individual has to develop his or her own philosophy on sensuality and sexuality. As you get older, your philosophies may change based on experiences, the situations and age.

It's up to parents to prepare their children for sexual choices they will have to make, because the school or the church are not ultimately responsible to deal with the subject. It has to be addressed with the parents, the grandparents and within the family. Children usually do what you do. You can talk all you want to, but they watch, and they see the love and affection that is shown between the family members. I would like to see a lot of talk about this subject, but most people are afraid to talk about it. I talked to my children about it at an early age. My wife and I were prepared for it. We let our daughters know that there were going to be menstrual periods, and we let our sons know that when it came along he didn't get a period, his sisters were going to be having them and what the process was. I taught biology and physical education; I coached girls and boys, and I knew when they had periods. I knew better than they did. If you have been honest and fair with your kids from day 1, and you know how you want to raise them, you won't have trouble talking to them. If you don't talk to them, they will get information from others, and then their get distortions and misinformation.

The ignorance out there on this subject is astronomical. I taught sex education to freshmen in a wellness class, and the ideas that they came in with were amazing, to say the least. They didn't even know about their own anatomy, much less the anatomy of the other person. They didn't know about biological phases that their bodies would be going though. when parents talk to their children about these things, they have to be knowledgeable themselves. You can't teach what you don't know.

The thought police

The thought police are thinking taboos that society has put on us. There are certain sexual things that you don't do; don't even think about it. A guy just can't get into ladies clothes and walk down the street. You have what they call kinky sex (sodomy, oral sex). Most of these acts are on the books as being crimes against nature. There certain things that certain religions tell you that you cannot do in a sexual realm. In any type of sexual relationship, I think it should be left up to the two consenting adults individuals. In some states, however, that can get you 20 years in jail.

A developing philosophy about it is if it doesn't hurt anyone, if it's discreet, and if it's between consenting adults, then it's OK. There is nothing taboo. There is nothing that can be examined. Think about it and come up with your own conclusion. Identify the worst case scenarios. What is the worst thing that could happen if you think about that happening? What you find out is that you grow. You cannot have infinite processing if you've got thought police and your stuck within the box.

We're always trying to look for truth, whatever it is. Truth changes too. As our abilities to interpret things evolve, we find that what was true 20 years ago is not true now. We've taking it to another level, and that's the way you want to live your life. Every day you get up, you know that something new is happening. Something else is out there to be created, and you're going to have fun creating in all of the various aspects of your life. Creating is a most pleasurable adventure.

Wherever your passions lie, that's what you should do. You owe it to yourself to be sensual. You owe it to yourself to be able to give pleasure. You owe it to yourself to be able to receive pleasure. You should always be discreet. That's basically a philosophy. I have not tried to give people answers; I've tried to make them think. I've just given people what's out there. They have to find the answers for themselves, but they also have to realize that there's a paradox because there aren't many everlasting answers. There are just choices, and after you made those choices you have to evaluate them to see if they were in your best interest. I always like win-win situations.

When you get to lifestyles in the sexual realm, you have a movement going on between gay and lesbian couples getting health care and other workers' social benefits. You also have lesbian couples adopting or having babies, and older women having children through vitro fertilization and embryo implantation. All of this raises the question that if they raise a male child, how do they teach them how to be male? If 2 gay men want to raise a child, a girl or a boy, how do they relate to that child in their sexuality and their sensuality? There are problems that are going to exist. Most everybody's family (if you want to look in the closet) over time has this problem one way or the other. Now I won't say it's a problem, but we have this situation and we have to ask ourselves, is it in some ways part of the natural order of things?

Nature versus nurture

We also have theories about what we call environment and heredity. You inherit some traits. You are predisposed genetically to certain things. What happens when you have that situation and there are youngsters being raised? For instance, if the mother is a truck driver and the husband is a househusband, and he decides that he wants to stay home and take care of the kids and the wife goes off to work. Let's say, for argument's sake, that they have a boy and a girl. How does that play out in the personalities and tendencies of the children? Will the little boy be more domestic? Will the girl be like her mother and take a more traditionally male-oriented career path? All of these things have to be thought about when you choose your style of living, and these are some questions that I don't think government or laws will be able to answer. I think it depends upon the individuals. Laws will go on the books to regulate behavior because that's why we have statutes and laws – to protect the rights of the individual, and to protect the rights of groups. That is determined in a court of law.

Spiritual sex

There are different levels of what I call sexiness, and some of it is for pleasure, some is for procreation, and then there's what we call "spiritual sex." Spiritual sex is when you know that you're going to a place that only the two of you can go, and you've never been there and are not likely to go with anybody else. Bells ring and chimes peal, and you just know that this is how it should be. It doesn't get any better than that. That's why we call our partner our "soul mate." That doesn't mean that he or she's going to be your only soul mate, or that it's going to feel that way all the time, but at least it lets you know what's possible. Unless you know what's possible, you might think what you've got is good. There are all levels and the levels and the levels and levels never end. Infinite processing. Infinite sexuality.

Some things to do

1. Assess your sex life with your partner.
2. Are there problems in your sex life?
3. Talk with your sexual partner about how he/she evaluates your satisfaction.
4. Write out and practice ways you can enhance your sex life.
5. Think of ways in which you can discuss your sexual philosophy with your children and write them down. (Very important!)
6. Go to the library. Talk with the librarians. Get online. Do research
7. Find a good coach.
8. Do what you want to do!

Chapter 13

SPIRITUALITY

Define it first

Webster's Dictionary definition of spirituality is "relating to, consisting of, or affecting the spirit; relating to sacred matters." It's a religious feeling that originates out of the unknown. The experts who are spiritual leaders go a little further than the dictionary in defining it. They deal with an essence of life that is ethereal – it cannot be felt, it's not tangible, but it exists. I'm going to look at it from that perspective also, but I'd like to make it a little bit personal.

My own definition of spirituality is that we are all one. We must go back to the beginning. Usually when I speak of something, I always try to go back to the N.O.O.T.: The time when there was nothing - that didn't exist before we were physical, before we were mental, and before we were spiritual. Through some phenomenon, the universe was created. I'm not trying to define that. I'm not saying I know what that is. I know that I exist in a physical form, but I also think I exist in a spiritual form, and I think that spiritual form is in the essence of what I call "God," and what was, is, and always will be. I'm not sure that what we call physical is physical in the perfect sense of physicality. We might be in a spiritual form in another realm acting out those spiritual ideas in the only way that we can – physically on earth. I know that's a little "way out," but somewhere in a spiritual form, I believe I exist. I also exist in a physical form, but the spirit cannot act out because, as my principal used to say, "It has no arms or legs." I do. When you think about the fact that we're living here on a big ball in the middle of nowhere, spinning around in the universe, it's mind-blowing. When you think about it, it has to be from some phenomenon that is not human. That is what I call "God." That is what I call spirituality. I don't think we'll ever fully understand it, but you can get close and closer so that you can live with it. What I speak of, I live with it. When I speak of spirituality, that is the realm in which I'm speaking. The spiritual manifests the physical.

All of life is paradox

You have to come up with your own philosophy of what spirituality is. How do you explain your existence? How do you communicate with the infinite being or infinite spirituality? That's up to you. You either believe it or you don't believe it, which brings us to what I call the universal paradox: All of life is a paradox. You've got to be able to look at 2 diametrically opposing views and realize that, in certain instances, they both may be right. I know that's inconsistent with our mathematical logic and theory, but I've found, as I've talked to people, as I've studied, and as I've lived, that there are some things that transcend logic. With the type of rationale that you could probably use mathematically and theoretically to prove God exists or spirituality exists, you could probably take the same point and turn in around and prove that they do not exist. It comes down to a matter of faith in what you believe. I believe faith is (ecclesiastically) proof – not proof, but belief in things unseen. There's an old proverb that says, "Faith is believing in something that does not exist until it does exist." I think that, from a spiritual realm to a physical realm, you first think about something, and after you've thought about it, you speak it or you write it. If you can believe that, you'll find a way to make that actually exist. I believe the purpose of living is to create things from a spiritual realm to a physical realm. At one time, before creation, nothing except God existed. If we can get over the idea of earthly beginnings and endings, it's not too difficult to conceptualize. It's abstract. Get away from beginnings and endings and go to the fact that these things can happen because of your thought processes. "Everything is created out of thought, and if you can think it, you can write it, you can say it, and you can believe it, then it can occur."

I don't think there are many impossibilities – though there may be improbabilities. We simply are limited in our thoughts and our creative abilities to make things happen. I think that we will always exist, we have always existed, and we probably will always exist as long as we think we will. In order to grow spirituality, you have to have ideas and concepts. Usually that's brought about in the home, the school, the church, and the neighborhood. Those concepts are passed down from parents as part of the culture of heritage. I'm not speaking about spirituality from the standpoint of the church, or the synagogue, or the tabernacle. I'm talking about individual spirituality that exists primarily between you and the spiritual world, which I will call God, or you can call Allah, or whomever. The first has to be a one-on-one relationship between you and whomever you choose as your spiritual mentor. You have to be taught at an early age about certain things that exist in the culture because, if not, you won't have a frame of reference to turn to once you run into problems.

When you are young, you were probably indoctrinated into certain faiths. You had no choice. As you get older and you read and you think and you interact with people who are of different faiths, you see some good things and some things that you question. Ultimately, it all becomes a matter of that last definition: what is it that you believe? What is it that you know deep down without coercion from the "thought police?" When you think out of the box, and when you're allowed to think freely without any fear, punishment, heresy or insecurity, just what have you found to be truth? You have to seek your own, because you cannot be really healthy until you do seek. Once you find it, you can still experience those things within the church and other faith-based organizations that you participate in, because we are social beings. You should understand that, within the context of those things, there are going to be some things that you don't believe in. I'm not saying that you should point that out to people because they have to find their own truth, but I think spiritually, you have to have that conversation in the morning, in the afternoons, with your "other self" – perhaps your alter ego. I don't know who or what it is, but when I start to talk spiritually and to meditate, somehow or other I'm into contact with another realm of my being. I'm not saying that anybody else would find that; I'm just saying, try it sometime. I'm not trying to give answers or prove anything. I'm not trying to indoctrinate anybody in any way. I'm just trying to say be truthful to yourself; realize that you didn't create this, and ask yourself how you can reconcile the fact that it exists.

What is your spiritual philosophy?

You have to have some kind of philosophy (a series of basic beliefs that you value and use for guidance) on the subject. If that makes you happy and comfortable, fine. As you grow older, you're going to find that, through "infinite processing," as soon as you reach a certain point, another idea is going to pop up and you're going to feel uncomfortable again. You've got to continue resolving. That's what life is. Every individual has to define his or her own spirituality and philosophy about a Supreme Being, spiritual force, or those things that you can't explain or control, and if you can get in touch with that, it adds a richness to your life.

We all have philosophies (whether we know it or not). What is yours grounded on? Usually a philosophy should be grounded on what I call universal truths: what is good for everybody on the earth? Then ask yourself what the experts say. Then examine your community, and then go within yourself, because you've got to interact with all of the above. You've got the family to deal with; you've got the community to deal with; you have the social order or the state; and you have the universal law to deal with.

You have to look at it from all four standpoints because, usually if you deal with the universal philosophy, it will serve most everybody best. When you go to the national or statewide level, it will be for those particular people, and then when you get to your community and your family, it takes in a smaller number of people. Hopefully we should be able to see how we function in each one of those categories because, in some instances, you'll find that you agree with this particular group, but you don't agree with another group.

Your philosophy may change depending on who you are and where you are, but you should have a core philosophy that you believe in, and that should be something that you've looked at from the personal, the international, the national, the local, and the community scenes. From these, you have crafted a philosophy, realizing that as you go out into the other realms, your basic philosophy wouldn't change, but you will be better able to understand where other philosophies are coming from. There needs to be a fair amount of tolerance in recognizing that everybody has potentially different philosophy.

If you define what's really best, it's what best for everybody. You are not living for everybody. You have certain things that you have to deal with and you have to reconcile those things. The main purpose of this book is to get people to think about where they're coming from. First, to define where they're coming from, and then to look at these aspects of their philosophies.

Take time to think about it

Today, people are so busy. Technology has moved everything so fast that everybody's flying on the holidays or e-mailing, and very seldom do you get time. I take time, at night and in the morning. – when I go to bed and when I get up – to just examine everything from the day's perspective and just think about it. It takes you 15-30 minutes to go to sleep. During that time, you can meditate on various aspects of your life to see what happened: that day was good, what was bad, what you should have done, what you didn't do. Think about it and talk to whoever your Spiritual Being is (I usually use the word God because that's inclusive in my culture; that's the way I was bought up). When you're thinking back to the events of the day, remember that everything bad happens to you is not bad for you. It's to teach you a lesson or steer you to another path. Think of setbacks and defeats as ways in which you need to learn more. Look at them as chances to improve, not things that are detrimental. Often when I started off the day and its really going badly – things are not going right, and then I get frustrated – I start the day over. I just wipe the day off and say, "All right, the new day starts today at 2 p.m. Forget all that other stuff! I'm starting a new day." I'll start a new day anytime I feel like it. Think – adjust – adapt – and move on!

Growth is hard

Learning is not necessarily comfortable. Any growth or learning experience is going to be somewhat uncomfortable or threatening. I have a little acronym "CSE,' that stands for comfortable, simplistic efficiency, which means you can't daily put in 12-14 hours if you're just on a run here, there, everywhere. You have to find a level of comfortableness, and it's not the same every day. Some days you could do more, some days you can't. Once you reached a point where you have sustained uncomfortableness, you're going to suffer from stress and burn out or have a breakdown.

You have to work comfortably, and then you have to simplify what you are doing the best way you can to make it clear to everybody.

Then you want it to be efficient. You don't want to spend a lot of energy on something and find out you could have done it a little bit better. I want it to be as efficient as it could possibly be.

As far as change is concerned, I think we should welcome change, because everything changes. Everyday it's a different world. When you wake up the next morning, God is constantly creating. The earth is moving. The universe is expanding. It's not the same universe. New things are being created. We're finding new planets. God is creating, and He/She continuously changes. He/She changes in nanoseconds. We're that way, too. We want to reach a level of comfort and then that's that. We want to get a work philosophy where we can feel comfortable. That's alright too, if that's where you want to go, but you will find that there are always questions. God gave us choices; He/She didn't give us answers. That's why you have so many religions and ways of life, because everybody has choices. That's what makes America so great. We have choices. You put choices and freedom together and you've got an ideal society. That's why so many people are trying to get over here. I think that we should welcome creativity. We should welcome change. It doesn't mean that we're always looking for it. If you look at what you did during the day when you go to bed at night, you can improve tomorrow. If it bothers you, you can improve or stay where you are. I'm not saying that you have to continue to create, but God creates through us because God doesn't have any arms and legs.

Everything that's going to be created here is going to have to be done by us. I think that creativity is the real essence of being. You are creating yourself right now, just like I'm creating myself, and the more you come in contact with different people things, the better person you can create for yourself.

<u>A never-ending cycle</u>

I don't think creation ends. This is an eternal game. I think I will come back again, and again, and again as many times as I chose to. I will assume another body. Maybe I will go to another level of physical being, but I don't think I will ever cease to be a person unless I chose to. I think that if I should chose that – I say, "Well, I want to stop here. I want to stay in my spiritual realm, and I don't want to take on a physical presence." See how infinite choice is?

The mere fact that we can do something, we can experience what we are thinking, I think that's what makes the spiritual, physical, mental, and all these others realms real or dynamic. It's a game. It's a never-ending game. It's one that you can do because that's what you think you can do. My thoughts are just as good as anybody else's. Who can tell me what I can think? I have free thoughts, and free mind, and free will. So if I think this, who's to tell me I'm wrong? If I want to live forever, then I'll live forever. When I die, I will just shed my body. My spirit and my soul will live eternally, and I will move into another level of existence. I won't have all the answers. I think that's why the universe was created. God did create us, and He created us for Him/Herself. We are His/Her creation, and He might be our creator. But God has always existed in spiritual form. If He did come down as Jesus (there are no impossibilities when you're talking from the spiritual realm) then spirit was indeed made flesh.

Usually we are bought up in some faith. That's a good starting point. You start out there. Also, when you think about your existence (your experience while you're here, and your experience after you leave here) there are certain moral obligations that society thinks that we should deal with if we're talking about it in a practical realm. In the Christian and Judaic religions, it starts off with the Ten Commandments and you look at those as sort of ways of living.

The spiritual life is a virtual way of living when you are dealing with yourself and the people around you. I was bought up in the Christian faith, but there's a book by Houston Smith called *The Seven Basic Religions,* and I would implore people to get that book. It deals with every one of them – all the main religions – the basic religions that there are. It's not heavy reading, but it explains the philosophies of the main religions. One of the spiritual needs of everybody is to live forever. Everybody wants to live forever. At some point in time, you realize that you're going to have to leave this body here. Nobody has escaped with it yet (maybe Joshua or Ezekiel in the wheel) but those things will come into your being. How did I get here? Where did I come from, and where am I going? Once you look at those things, these are spiritual questions because you're not going to take this body with you. Once you start trying to resolve those things, you will start asking questions. One of the best places to find the answers to that questions is a book called *The Religions of Man*, which discusses all of the major and known religions. It even goes back to before there was structured religion, and it tells you what things man has always wanted to have or do. He's always wanted wealth, but even when he got wealth, he never had enough because the wealth wouldn't change him to another being, and he couldn't take it with him. Those questions will always be there. I would think that a person who's trying to learn will go there first, if they really wanted to know, and then see history all the way up through the ones that they have and then look at the one that they are in, or if they are not in one.

There also is a discussion on atheism, if you do not believe. If you don't believe, what is it that you do believe? You've got to believe in something. It might not be in religion; it might not be in God. It might be in science, but regardless of how you explain it, everything breaks down with the big bang. Steven Hawking, who's one of the world's greatest physicists, has said that there was a big bang. All the experts said that there was a creation, and that may or may not be so, but it exists and in the physical world, things have a beginning and they have an ending. Where do you fit in the realm of things? A lot of people don't think about these things. Think, think, and rethink.

Going too far with spirituality

We know that some people get out of balance with spirituality. They become obsessed. I would think probably a case like Jim Jones and the cults and maybe the Branch Davidians, although I'm not saying they did. It was all right for them. It would not have been all right for me. I'm not trying to put a limit on how far you can go or how far you can process. That's left up to you, but if you look at your life and how it affects you and how it affects other people around you, if you are making other people better (it's sort of like an athlete, a good athlete makes his teammates better). It's not about how good he is. He's able to bring the team along- to make everybody else play better. Wherever you go, people will like to be around you because you make them feel and perform better.

Usually, when you go to extremes, at some point you're out there but you lost contact with the common people. Jesus was always with the common people. He always was able to relate to them. He always had ways in which he could teach them and make them feel better. That's what this book is for: to make you a better person.

Individually, I think you have a right to go where you want to go, no matter what it might appear to be to other people. You might be a fanatic; you might be whatever you want to be. If you're happy in that, fine. When you start to negatively affect other people, then I think you might need to check it. It's also up to the other person to tell you that you're all right, but you take that over there or keep it with yourself because I don't want any part of it. It disturbs me. You can sit down and show them that it might be right for you, but's it's not right for me. That's okay if it's all right for you. You see, usually, if something is good for the international community, it's good for the immediate community. Just because something is good for the immediate community does not mean it's good for the broader population. If there's a conflict, usually the international philosophy is going to be really be the sort of benchmark. You got to look at the way people have been socialized.

Some people need the church and other organizations because they don't have those skills to do that. I'm not saying that everybody shouldn't be individualistic or people shouldn't be in cults. I'm not saying any of that. Whatever you feel comfortable with, that's where you should go. The structures that have passed on for years and years in organized religions are going to still exist. It's a great thing. I'm a member of a church and I go, but still, individually, I have my own thoughts about spiritual things, and there are some things that I don't discuss personally with anybody because the way that they're structured, it would create some needless problems for me and them.

In the end, life is all a paradox. How can something be created from nothing? It can, if you believe it can. Faith is believing in something that isn't so until it is so. Just be whatever you want to be.

- Thoughts
- Beliefs
- Words of affirmation
- Faith
- Action
- The creation process

Some things to do

1. Write out your philosophy on spirituality.

2. Visit a faith based place of worship other than your own.
3. Converse with people of faith different from your own.
4. Give a copy of this book to a faith based library to keep on reserve.
5. Talk with a librarian. Get online. Do research.
6. Find a good coach.
7. Do what you want to do.

CHAPTER 14

MAKING IT ALL WORK TOGETHER

ABOUT now, you may be thinking, "Coach, there are an awful lot of new ideas in this book. How in the world can I remember all of them?" My wife and I developed the concepts and philosophies in these chapters and it took us a number of years, and we had to develop our own way of remembering them. After all, we're telling you that you need to consider the state of every critical element of your life on a regular basis.

We have always found that it helps to make up an acronym or some other easy ways to remember things, so a few years ago, we developed one for the process: we tell ourselves every day to:

"Keep the emphasis on the SPEMPP-FAR-SIS."

"Spempp-far-sis" is one of my many made-up words, but it's very useful to me. each letter stands for one of the Real Daily Dozen. It's a mnemonic acronym.

- **S-** Social matters
- **P-** Physical matters
- **E-** Education
- **M-** Mentality
- **P-** Politics
- **P-** Professional matters
- **F-** Financial matters
- **A** - Attitude
- **R-** Relationships
- **S-** Sexuality
- **I** - Imagination
- **S-** Spirituality

Each one, reach one, teach one: Emphasis on the SPEMPP-FAR-SIS

Now that we have this system, we find that is much easier to check in on various elements of our SPEMPP-FAR-SIS. My family understood the term, because we might tell them my SPEMPP-FAR-SIS is off today. My students heard it enough times to understand it, too. I'm offering it up as one easy way to remember what's really important. Whatever system you use, make it easy so you'll use it every day.

Conclusion

IN the beginning of this book, I told you what it wasn't: not a typical self-help book, or a health book, not a philosophy book, or religious book. Yes, it covers all of the topics, but the point has been to make you think, not to give you answers. You may agree with many of the concepts here, or you may violently disagree. That's OK. The point is that you're thinking about them. God gave us choices, not answers.

When you first started reading, you may have thought you didn't have any philosophies about the topics covered. You may have thought your philosophies were different other than they are now that you explored them. The point is that you have a philosophy about things and you need to recognize it. It will guide you in so many ways. Before you read this book, you may have been hard working at a job you didn't enjoy, just earning enough money to buy things that you didn't even care about. You have been busy raising children without really thinking about how you were shaping them for the rest of their lives. You have been one of the millions of Americans who sleep walk through their lives. Stop that.

The point of this book is we all have to be accountable for our lives. Not only do we need to do right things, but we also need to learn, grow, contribute to, and enjoy our lives continuously.

Every day, in every way, you are getting better, and better, and better. Keeping the emphasis on the SPEMPP-FAR-RSIS is one way of doing that.

Please give as many books to as many people as you can financially afford to. Start with your family, neighbors, co-workers, and family members of other ethnic groups. Then give it to strangers that you think might profit from them.

It is most beneficial to you that you give your spouse or significant other a copy of this book. Do not give him or her your copy.

After you both have finished reading it, sit down at times and discuss each chapter. Discuss your family philosophies with other family members and members of other ethnic groups that have read the book. Invite people of other ethnics groups to lunch and sit down and discuss different philosophies. If you are comfortable with them, invite them and their families over for a cook out or family dinner. This should give you a starting point from which to improve race relations. It should go a long way in in letting you know about racial fears and prejudices.

HARVEY D. HEARTLEY, SR.

Recommended Reading

Books and Their Authors

1. *Men are From Mars, Women are From Venus* by Dr. John Gray
2. *The Religious Man* by Huston Smith
3. *Passages* by Gail Sheehy

About The Author

HARVEY D. HEARTLEY, SR.

HARVEY DELAFONTE HEARTLEY, SR., affectionately nicknamed "Coach," was born on October 22, 1934 to the late Matthew and Lucille Heartley. He was raised in Clayton, North Carolina with his brothers Matthew (deceased) and Alfred. They were devoted members of First Baptist Church.

Upon graduation from Johnston County Training School in Smithfield, North Carolina, Harvey attended North Carolina College in Durham, North Carolina. He received a BS in

Biology and an MS in Physical education. Later, he attended North Carolina State University in Raleigh, North Carolina where he completed all requirements for a doctoral degree with the exception of the dissertation.

Coach started his professional coaching career at Cooper High School in Clayton, North Carolina in 1956, transitioning to Ligon High School in Raleigh, North Carolina through 1968, winning tennis and basketball championships. Later in 1968, the late Governor Dan K. Moore appointed him as Youth Coordinator of Sports for the state of North Carolina. His passion for coaching led him to join St. Augustine's College "Mighty Falcons" where he faithfully served as associate professor, director of athletics, head men's basketball, fencing, and golf coaches. Coach Heartley also served for many years as project administrator of the NCAA national youth summer program, where he mentored many young athletes. He invested over thirty years of his coaching career to shaping the lives of staff, students and athletes, taking many athletes overseas to participate in international athletics. He was fondly referred to as the "Father of Falcon Athletics." Recognizing his outstanding contribution to athletics, Coach Heartley was inducted into the CIAA, NCCU, and St. Augustine College Basketball Hall of Fame, CIAA Coach of the Year, 4 time CIAA Athletic Director of the Year, and NAIA District 26 Coach of the Year.

Among the many accolades and positions Harvey held in the community, he was a lifetime member of Kappa Alpha Psi Fraternity, served on the Board of Directors of the Meadowbrook Country Club and the Boys Club of Raleigh, Investron, YMCA of Garner Road, former president of Raleigh/Wake NCCU Alumni Association and a member of AARP, Chapter 5032 of Southeast Raleigh, North Carolina.

Harvey D. Heartley, Sr. passed away June 23, 2014. He is survived by his wife, Maria; stepson, Gregory; his three children, Delphyne, Harvey Jr. (Mary), and Shawn (Eddy); Anna G. Harkley, mother of his children; his brother, Alfred (Beverly); four grandchildren, Antoine (Desne), Haley, Sydney, Natalie; one great-grandchild, Aniya; and a host of nieces, nephews, cousins, relatives and friends.

In his honor, St. Augustine's University in Raleigh, North Carolina has started a scholarship fund. To make contributions, send them to:

The Harvey D. Heartley, Sr. Scholarship Fund
c/o St. Augustine's University Office of Development
1315 Oakwood Avenue
Raleigh, North Carolina 27610

www.ingramcontent.com/pod-product-compliance
Lightning Source LLC
Chambersburg PA
CBHW071157160426
43196CB00011B/2104